PETERBOROUGH:

PLEASE SLOW DOWN

A panorama view of Peterborough, c. 1960

PETERBOROUGH

PLEASE SLOW DOWN

Michael Moore
(edited by Tess Livingstone)

The Publisher's Apprentice

The Publisher's Apprentice
An imprint of Connor Court Publishing Pty Ltd
Copyright © Michael Moore 2014

PO Box 224W
Ballarat VIC 3350
sales@connorcourt.com
www.connorcourt.com

ISBN: 9781925138443 (pbk.)

Cover design by Maria Giordano

Printed in Australia

CONTENTS

Dedicated to the memory of
Rosemary (Posy) Durham
1928-2004

Lovely place is Curdies River, at its entrance near the sea

In my memory's seat forever, dearest thou shalt be to me

There my home with fare so humble should a stranger call to see

With our best will make him welcome, in our cottage by the sea.

Pretty place is Curdies River, though unnoticed it has been

Here all nature clothed in splendour in magnificence is seen

Time steals on – when on this river many a happy face will see

Reflections of a wondrous future near our cottage by the sea.

Up and down this lovely river, Thornley's party have surveyed

Causing homes for many strangers all along the track they made.

Pleasant place is Curdies River on its banks we soon shall see

Homesteads for our sons forever from our cottage by the sea.

James Meek

Peterborough

by A.E. Brown

Oft on a bright and sunny day, when tourists come and go,
Watching the many scenes of wrecks in the long, long ago,
There is a nook not far away, battered by many a gale,
Here lies that beautiful sailing barque, the *Falls of Halladale*.

The full rigged ship the *Schomberg* wrecked many years ago,
It was here at Peterborough, where the Curdies Inlet flows,
It was here that some old pioneers prepared to make their home,
Away out in the wilderness beside the ocean foam.

There some had reared their families, and some had gone away,
But when it comes to pioneers, well, they are the ones that stay,
Their friendship everlasting, as many a tourist knows,
You will always get a welcome where the Curdies Inlet flows.

Peterborough History Time Line

1839 *Children* wrecked at Childers Cove.

1843 *Skipjack* wrecked near Bold Projection.

1845/6 Charles La Trobe expeditions to the Otway Ranges

1855 Prospector Mr J.M. Meek, after arriving by sea in his yacht, sank a well on the corner of Robertson and Irvine. This was a base for prospecting for gold in the Otways. He did not find gold, but good country. He explored the Gellibrand and went 12 miles up the Curdies by boat. Meek alerted the Government and the public to the value of the land and the rivers.

1855 *Schomberg* wrecked – aborigines seen wearing two left foot Wellington boots and crinoline dresses.

1858 *John Scott* wrecked near Flaxman's Hill – 14 February.

1863 James Meek producing hermetically sealed fish at Peterborough.

Crossing Curdies River

Peterborough township c. 1950

1864 Lifeboat wrecked near the spit – Mr Hall and Captain Seilly drowned

1864 James Meek's gold seeking expeditions to the Otways. C.F. Wilkinson of Victorian Geological Survey Department says no prospect of gold in the Otways.

1865 Meek, Dr James, Foote and Williams explore up Curdies River to Terang

1865 The Parish of Narrawaturk was established and section A was marked on the survey map for a township. This was on the west side of the river and took in Meek's hut and well. The township was surveyed by Nathan Thornley, an associate of Robert Hoddle surveyor of the City of Melbourne.

1866 Thornley's township survey was completed into 94 lots and the place named Peterborough. Some land was sold in Warrnambool. The first titles issued.

1866 Cobb & Co ran coaches from Warrnambool to Melbourne three times a week. Ceased after the railway extended in 1889.

1868 James Irvine (the First) and son William settled at the Bay of Islands Farm.

1873 Charles and Jessie MacGillivray established their home at *Oak Bank*, on the eastern bank of Curdies Inlet, Peterborough-Timboon Road. Margaret Euphemia (Effie) MacKenzie was born on 14 December at *Oak Bank*.

1874 Jemima V. Robertson (née Cumming), of *Connewarren* Hexham acquired a 14 acre property in Peterborough. She built a holiday home on a site on the corner of Blair Street and Robertson in 1875. This became known as *The Big House*. The original owner of this property was Samuel McGregor. John Langabeer, a fisherman, and his wife were the first caretakers.

1875 Jemima Robertson gave 2.5 acres of land on the corner of Hamilton and Irvine for a church and also a block of 40 acres on the Warrnambool Road. Charles MacGillivray was secretary/treasurer of the Presbyterian Church Committee.

1876 Margaret Hamilton of Mortlake built Hamilton's Cottage on the corner of Mac's and Irvine.

1877 *Young Australian* wrecked off front beach. Captain James Robilliard in charge of salvage operations.

1878 *Loch Ard* wrecked (June).

1878 *Napier* wrecked – Port Campbell inlet – September.

1879 Robert Blair family came to live north of *Oak Bank* on Peterborough-Timboon Road.

1880 Jessie MacGillivray's grandfather, Andrew Macdonald, came to live at *Oak Bank*. He became unofficial postman. He collected mail from Port Campbell and delivered to Peterborough.

1880 First meeting about establishing a school held at *The Big House.*

1881 Amended scale of fees for Shires of Hampden and Warrnambool operated ferry across the Curdies at Peterborough. Foot passengers 3d, Horse or cattle 1s, vehicle drawn by horse 1s, vehicle drawn by 2 horses 1/6, loads greater than one ton 2s, merchandise 1d per hundredweight. Teddy Oarr for some years operated the ferry. Shire of Hampden refused to pay the account.

1882 Mail service from Port Campbell to Peterborough established, via *Oak Bank.*

1882 Trader *Hannah Thompson* arrived Port Campbell.

1883 Railway extended to Camperdown.

1882 70 children at the one teacher school at Port Campbell.

1884 James Irvine (the second) became caretaker of *The Big House* following the death of Jemima Robertson.

1884 The Shire of Warrnambool rate book has James Arthur Robilliard paying the rates on 642 and 490 acres at Peterborough. This would include most of Jemima Robertson's Peterborough farm and in 1896 he purchased her 700 acres from the Bank of Australasia. Robilliard married 17-year-old Helen (Nelly) Beckett in 1879. They had 10 children. Three of their sons were to become farmers in the district.

1885 School for Peterborough district children built at Wallaby Hill at the junction of Boundary and Timboon Roads. It was part time and run in conjunction with the Nirranda Settlement School. Belle Anderson, later operator of the Strawberry Gardens farm, was a student there.

1885 Wooden Presbyterian church built by Moreland of Port Campbell. Cost £66.8s, corner of Hamilton and Irvine,

Panorama, 1940, looking east from sandhill

1885 Marram grass planted on foreshore, to arrest sand drift, following fires to eradicate rabbits.

1887 Syndicate of three men (including James Irvine 2nd) built *Peterborough House* on the corner of Mac's and Irvine.

1887 Railway extended to Terang

1889 December, Robert Blair enlarged his home on the east side of the river and opened it as a guest house.

1889 Railway extended to Warrnambool

1890 School opened in Presbyterian church at Peterborough – 10 pupils, Langabeers 3, Irwins 2, Sparks 3 and Irvines 2.

1891 First race meeting held at Two-Mile Bay Racecourse.

1892 Railway Camperdown to Timboon (The Black Stump) – completed 5 April. Daily train and mail service.

1892 August: *Newfield* wrecked east of the Crown of Thorns. Government petitioned to open post office.

1893 The Peterborough Post Office re-established at *Sunny Brae* in Sarah Macdonald's house with Charles MacGillivray as the Post Master.

Margaret Irvine and John Irvine at the bridge opening in 1987. John is the brother-in-law of Margaret whose husband Bill Irvine was deceased at this time. They are in the back seat of Elizabeth Irvine's Austin 7 car called "The Flea" which was famous in Peterborough

1894 Helen Blair (married woman) obtains title to the late Jemima Robertson's property in Blair Street from her executors William Armstrong and Alexander Dundas Robertson.

1894 School at Wallaby Hill closed due to lack of numbers

1897 Hampden Shire re-establishes ferry service erecting a bell on the east bank of the Curdies. One gong for the Irvine's Hotel two gongs for the *Tulach Ard* Guest House.

1898 F.L. Harding bought the business of coaches from Timboon to Peterborough from Mrs E.J. Morehouse.

1900 Tom MacKenzie marries Effie MacGillivray.

1901 Port Campbell Rifle Club formed and rifle range used at Two Mile Bay.

1903 *Peterborough House* changed to *Peterborough Hotel.*

1904 Golf Club formed at Peterborough.

1904 Tom and Effie McKenzie moved from Inglewood, north of Port Campbell, to Hamilton's Cottage when Tom tendered successfully for the mail contract between Peterborough and Timboon. Tom established a successful coaching business and bought several blocks of land in Peterborough.

1905 Mr Good conducts successful two acre agricultural experiment between Peterborough and Port Campbell.

1908 Tom McKenzie built *Tulach Ard* in Mac's Street and moved into it.

1908 Hamilton's Cottage purchased by James Irvine and used as an annex to *Peterborough Hotel*. By this time there were *Tulach Ard, Sunny Brae, Blair Athol* and *Palmyra* (corner of Robertson and Blair) taking in guests. Over 200 visitors could be accommodated.

1908 *Falls of Halladale* wrecked – November.

1909 Tom McKenzie granted the coach licence for Timboon to Peterborough by the Cobden Court.

1910 Death of John Irvine, son of James Irvine (2nd), aged 22 years.

1912 State Governor, Sir Thomas Gibson-Carmichael, and Premier, Hon. John Murray, visit Peterborough.

1914 *Antares* wrecked – no survivors.

1914 First car came to Peterborough – severe drought.

1915/16 Mrs Jim Blair conducted a subsidised school in *Palmyra*. Students were Ballis children, Aila and Bet MacKenzie and Moyle Breton.

1919 Death of James Irvine – disappeared while crossing the river.

1924 Wooden Presbyterian church removed.

1925 *Falls of Halladale* house moved to Hamilton Street and *Moonya* built on corner of Irvine Road and Robertson Street.

*Thomas Donald MacKenzie, grandson of Thomas Ingles MacKenzie,
with ferry bell*

1926 Annette Breton purchases block from Helen Blair corner of Mac's and Blair.

1927 First timber bridge opened – cost £4872. Built by Roche Bros.

1927 Following the death of Helen Blair the previous year, Lily Ann Blair and Mary Jane Blair (spinsters) inherit her property.

1938 Irvines' lease *Peterborough Hotel* to John and Ruby Wiber following huge hail storm. Mary Weibye (Ruby Wiber's mother) purchased Hotel from Irvines in 1943.

1942 Twenty-four hour coastal watch established in hut built on Foreshore Reserve sand dunes west of the Ladies Beach.

1944 Miss Hautot, teaching nine students in Mechanics Hall, moved to Hotel in the winter months.

1946 Annual Sand Castle Competition revived by Kit Tinsley, prizes presented by Lady Dumfumblebee, Mayoress of Fumblefun (in drag).

1947 Betty Hession teaching pupils Joan Wiber, G. and K. MacKenzie, Sissons, Jarvis families, Barlings, L. Staghorn, Ray Lane and Jenny Irvine.

1951 Public tennis courts built at the Gap. Part funded from a legacy of £500 provided by Kit Tinsley.

1953 Hotel purchased by local syndicate, Desmond Moore, Tom Austin, Rod Calvert and A.W. (Wocca) Moore.

1955 December: Electricity switched on by Effie MacKenzie, oldest citizen.

1955 Jane Chirnside's 21st birthday party in *Karrawingi* marquee.

1956 Sturzaker's *Seagull Café* in Mac's Street burnt down.

1958 Hotel café and bar burnt down.

1958 Golf Club re-established in Rod Calvert's house corner Blair and Schomberg. Later Golf Club bought Ian (Boy) Armstrong's house in Schomberg Road following his death in a car accident. 1972 Title in name of N. Rod. Calvert and John Irvine, 1976 – J. Irvine & Peter Clark, 1990 – Golf Club.

1962 Wooden bridge at Peterborough widened.

1963 Will Kelly drowned near the Sand Slide.

1963 Jenkin's Store Mac's Street burnt down (Mac's Street west).

1964 700 hectare Port Campbell National Park gazetted.

1965 *Peterborough Hotel* burnt down.

1966 Town water supply connected.

1967 *Tulach Ard* and *Doo Drop Inn* burnt down (next to post office).

Bridge opening, 1987

1971 Foreshore Committee disbanded with management taken over by Council.

1987 New 11 span bridge opened – 30 October – cost $2,427,800.

1990 London Bridge fell down

Glossary

A few place names familiar to Peterborough residents that might puzzle newcomers.

Crazy Kate – the bay immediately to the north of the old Peterborough township. In some old maps it has been referred to as Wild Dog Cove. On the western side there is a large rock which was called Lion Rock because the top resembled the head of a lion, but the head has long since worn away. To the south east there is a small beach which was called Post Office Beach. This was once known for its large population of perriwinkles.

Crown of Thorns – a rock on the east end of Newfield Bay which was covered in sharp rocks projecting from the top. This rock was sitting loosely on a ledge near the water's edge, but was dislodged and broke in half.

Giant's Trousers – two adjacent holes in the rock near the former pathway to the Men's Pool.

The Crown of Thorns

London Bridge

Ladies Beach – the beach to the south of the Golf Club House. This beach and the small swimming hole were traditionally reserved exclusively for women to swim in the morning before breakfast.

London Bridge – a rock formation on the Great Ocean Road between Peterborough and Port Campbell which once had two connecting arches. The near arch collapsed in 1990.

The Arch – a rock feature to the east of Point Hesse and London Bridge. Once there were steps down the cliff known as Murray Steps and a tunnel exiting to a ledge on the east side of the arch.

Men's Pool – the rock pool to the south of the front beach. This pool was traditionally reserved exclusively for men to "skinny dip" before breakfast each morning.

Narrows – the north end of the Curdies Estuary where a large number of birds breed.

Sand Slide – the beach near Worm Bay where the cliff face was once covered in sand and children could slide down to the beach.

Strawberry Gardens – a farm growing strawberries prior to the Second World War. Located close to the Great Ocean Road near London Bridge. The farm supplied visitors with strawberries and cream.

The Arch from Murray Steps

Mens Pool

1

Uncovering the Great Ocean Road's
best kept secret

THREE hours drive from Melbourne, Peterborough is a coastal haven, west of the Twelve Apostles on the Great Ocean Road. The fortunate families who have holidayed there for generations know it is one of Victoria's best kept secrets. As Rosemary Durham, whose children are fourth generation residents, said: "If Peterborough is in your blood you can't escape. We have our own house where *Tulach Ard* (a former guest house) used to be and so the tradition goes on. My children are fourth generation, and Peterborough's charm continues; basically I hope it never changes …"

A quintessential storybook seaside village, Peterborough is blessed with safe, sandy beaches nestled between rugged limestone and ironstone cliffs. The rolling waves, sheltered coves and rockpools, abundant ocean and estuary fishing, beachside tennis courts, open parkland and breathtaking coastal walks delight children and adults. The upper reaches of the estuary is home to large numbers of birds. They nest in marshes in the area known as the "Narrows" and black swans swim on the estuary. The cliff top golf course is one of Australia's most picturesque.

This is the story of Peterborough from the earliest colonial times to the end of the 20th century. It is also a story of nation building, of industries, farms, homes and towns carved from a wilderness that promised much but took back-breaking effort to develop. It is about enterprising, hearty pioneers such as James Meek and Dr Daniel Curdie, who overcame the tyranny of distance without assistance and whose courage would seem almost unbelievable to the tens of thousands cosseted by the state in the age of entitlement.

Peterborough was named in the late 19th century, presumably after the East Anglican Cathedral town in Cambridgeshire. This is supposition, however, and the exact origin of the name is one of the town's abiding mysteries. Peterborough is sited between the Curdies Inlet and the Bay of Martyrs, on a strip known as the Shipwreck Coast. More than 400 shipwrecks occurred in the area in the 19th and early 20th centuries. The *Children* in 1839 and the *Schomberg* in 1855 were among the most famous. Exploring the remains of the wrecks is a popular past time for scuba divers.

Traditionally, Peterborough was part of the lands of the Kirrae Whurrrong Aboriginal people and home to the Baradh-gundig clan. Middens along the coast suggest an extensive number of sheltered campsites offered easy access to coastal reefs for shellfish. The precise number of Aborigines along the south coast at the time of white settlement is impossible to calculate. The population was heavily depleted by smallpox epidemics in 1830 and 1847, to which Aborigines had no immunity. An 1872 estimate by the Board for the Protection of Aborigines suggested the indigenous population was about 300, spread across Geelong and Colac 28, Camperdown 40, Warrnambool 51, Port Fairy 17, Framlingham 63 and Portland 100. A measles epidemic in 1878 wrought further devastation.

The first known white settlers of the area that was to become Peterborough ran about 2,500 cattle over 30,000 acres in the 1840s on what was known as Buckley's Creek run (west), extending from Childers Cove to the Curdies River, about 13 miles.

Buckley's Creek run (east), consisting of 12,800 acres, was based at Wallaby Creek to the north of Peterborough. J.E Dance

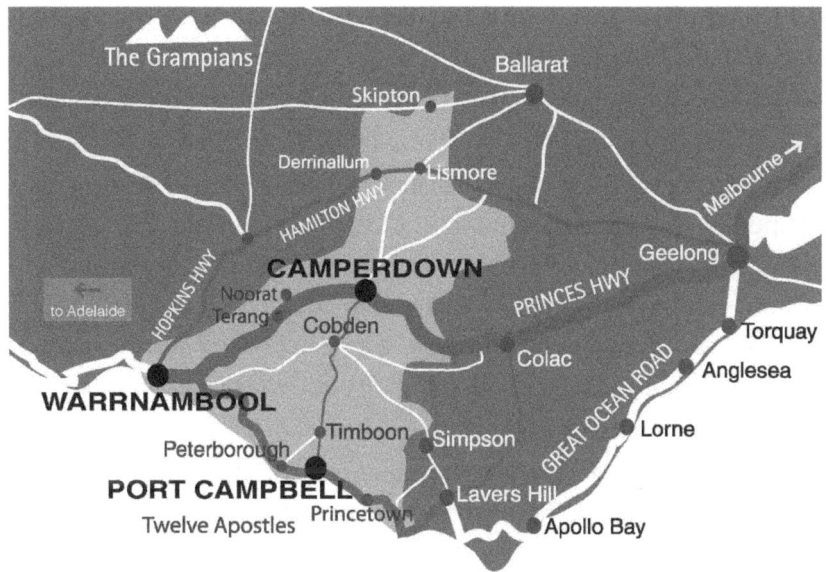

built cattle yards and a hut near the sand dunes on the east side of the Curdies River.

In 1868 the Irvine brothers, James and William, occupied the Bay of Island's Farm five miles west of Peterborough and Charles MacGillivray established *Oak Bank* in 1873 on the east side of the estuary.

The man recognised as Peterborough's first settler, English-born James McKain Archibald Job Meek, a former gold miner, sank a well and built a hut on the western side of the Curdies River mouth in 1855 on the corner of what is now Robertson Street and Irvine Road. Curdies Inlet had been named after Dr Daniel Curdie, a Scotsman who had established a pastoral enterprise in the district in 1840. Meek moved to Melbourne in 1859 after the failure of the "Tiger" fishing enterprise and returned in 1863, but he moved between Peterborough and Warrnambool.

The first house in Peterborough, known as *The Big House*, was built in Blair Street by Mortlake squatter Jemima Robertson in

1875. Within a year, John Langabeer and his wife had occupied it and were in Peterborough when the *Young Australian* was wrecked in 1877. The man who was to become one of Peterborough's most influential residents, James Irvine, opened a guesthouse in 1885.

Aside from its pioneer settlers, Peterborough's destiny was shaped by events in the Southern Ocean region in the 18th century. After the discovery of Bass Strait in 1798, when George Bass and Matthew Flinders circumnavigated Van Diemen's Land in the sloop *Norfolk*, a huge sealing industry was established on the islands north of Van Diemen's Land and the south-west coast of what was to become Victoria.

Thousands of seals were slaughtered for their oil and skins, years before John Batman arrived in Port Phillip in 1835. With the establishment of a convict settlement at Hobart Town in 1803, escaped convicts and others settled on the Bass Strait islands slaughtering seals. "A local breed of 'Straitsmen' grew up, a fearfully hardened race who raided the mainland coast to abduct native 'wives'," wrote historian Don Charlwood, best known for his memoir of his service in Bomber Command during World War II, *No Moon Tonight*. By about 1830 the seal population had been depleted and was replaced by a whaling industry based in Portland and Port Fairy. Henry Reed had a whaling station in Portland in 1833.

By 1837, only two years after explorer and grazier John Batman had arrived in Port Phillip, Port Fairy and Portland were thriving communities with hundreds of acres of land under cultivation. Edward Henty had settled in Portland with his four sons, Stephen, Thomas, John and Frank in 1834. Stephen ran the whaling business while the other brothers developed merino sheep and exported wool. Portland had a population in excess of 2,500 by 1843. Like Port Fairy, it was bolstered by immigration from Van Diemen's Land. Up to two thousand tons of whale oil was being exported until the 1860s when the whale numbers became depleted.

In contrast, Warrnambool's early settlers were predominantly graziers. Among the earliest were the Allen Brothers who established a cattle station on the Hopkins River at Allansford and Thomas Manifold at Grassmere. The Ware brothers, Jeremiah, Joseph and John had many large runs including, Wooriwyrite, Koort-Koort-nong, Native Creek, Yalla-y-Poora, Minjah and Barwidgee.

Contract surveyor, George Smythe, was engaged in 1847 to survey the coastline between the Hopkins River and Moonlight Head. The first Christian church in the Shire of Hampden was founded by a group of gentlemen of the Western District who used to meet on Sundays to hunt dingoes and enjoy a get-together at Davidson's Inn, Darlington, which was then known as Elephant Bridge. One man had the idea they should collect subscriptions and secure a clergyman to establish a Presbyterian church. The first formal meeting was held at Davidson's Inn on 8 February 1847, attended by James Webster, Daniel Curdie, Lachlan Mackinnon, Robert Anderson, Alexander Davidson, George Eddington, Thomas Brown and Niel Black. Donald Craig of Eddington and J.G. Ware of Wooriwyrite each gave 50 acres on the boundary of their stations for a manse. Building was in progress within a few weeks.

Rev William Hamilton was the first minister and his stipend began on 1 April 1847. He visited all the large sheep stations within an area of 50 miles, preaching in barns, woolsheds and private rooms to congregations seldom exceeding a dozen or 14. The manse was later destroyed by a fire and replaced with a large stone building. In 1852, a small church was built on the site – the Western Church of Kilnoorat – and it remained until 1880 when it was destroyed by a bush fire. Years after, a heap of rubble and an old mulberry tree, that would have been familiar to the early parishioners, were all that remained. A memorial perpetuated the memory of the founders.

Almost 30 years later, Margaret Hamilton had a holiday cottage built near the mouth of the Curdies River, in 1876. In her book *Sealing Sailing and Settling in South Western Victoria*, Bonnie MacKenzie recounted that her grandfather and his brother Duncan carted stones from the beach for the foundations of the cottage and cut shingles for the roof. When it was completed, Rev Hamilton held a service there, the first ever conducted by an ordained minister in the Peterborough district. "All the local people attended, even the irreverent Teddy Oarr," Bonnie MacKenzie wrote.

In 1864, Messrs J. Stanhope and McCreddin, the occupiers of Buckley's Creek run (west) and James Murray of Glenample and Joseph Dance of Buckley's Creek run (east) were notified by the Lands Department that their grazing licences had been cancelled to make way for a survey prior to sale by auction.

Nathan Thornley surveyed the township of Peterborough in 1865 and on 6 July 1866 *The Warrnambool Examiner* referred to the sale of town allotments at "Peterborough, Curdies Inlet." The area had previously been known as "Curdies Inlet" and this was one of the first times, if not the first time, the name "Peterborough" was mentioned.

By then, Peterborough was already famous for the number of shipwrecks on the nearby coast. The *Children* was wrecked at Childers Cove in 1839. Some of the survivors, looking for Port Fairy, walked the wrong way to the east before returning and probably were the first whites to traverse this area of coast. Later in 1845 and 1846, the Superintendent of Port Phillip District, Charles La Trobe organised expeditions from Allansford to Cape Otway with the objective of building a lighthouse. Eventually a lighthouse was built at Cape Otway in 1848. The *Skipjack* was wrecked in 1843, *Schomberg* in 1855, *John Scott* 1858, *Young Australian* in 1877, *Newfield* in 1892, *Falls of Halladale* in 1908 and *Antares* in 1914.

PART ONE

Pioneers

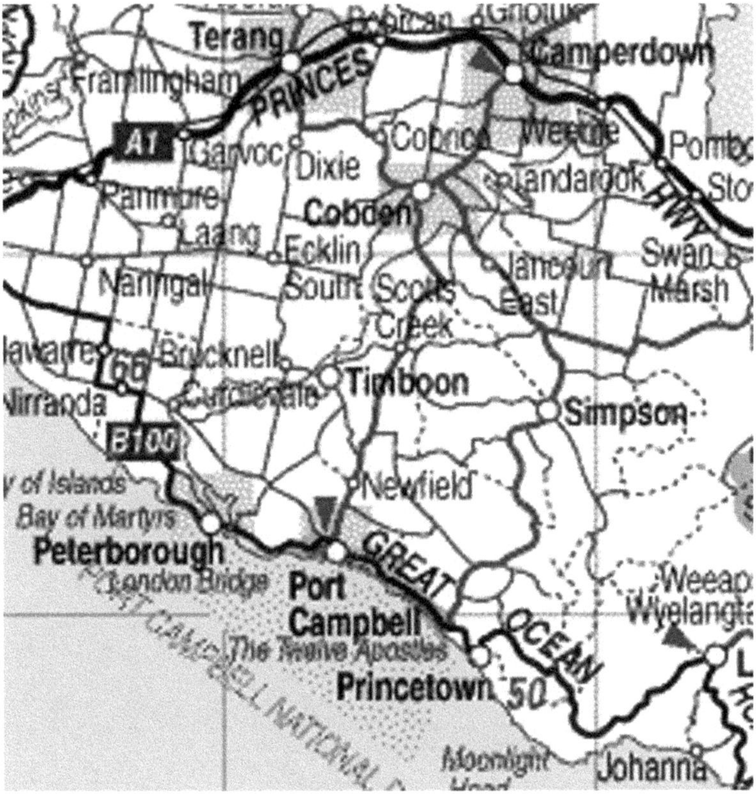

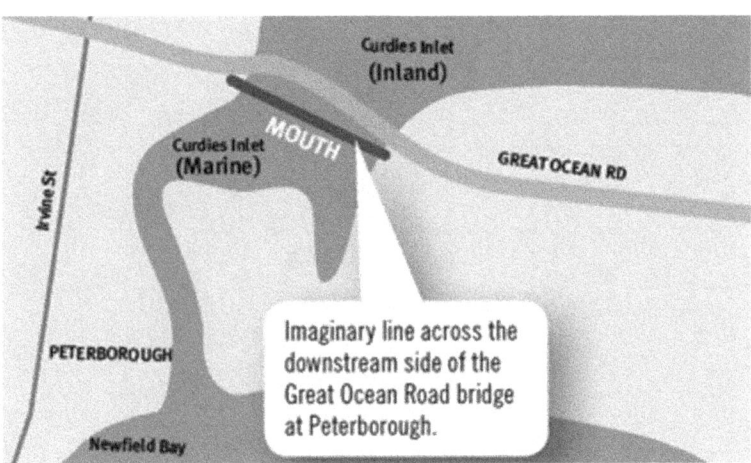

Terang
Camperdown
Framlingham
PRINCES
HWY
A1
Garvoc
Dixie
Cobrico
Weerite
Panmure
Laang
Cobden
Ecklin
South
Scotts
Creek
Jancourt
East
Swan
Marsh
Brucknell
Timboon
Simpson
B100
Newfield
Bay of Martyrs
Peterborough
London Bridge
Port
Campbell
GREAT
OCEAN
The Twelve Apostles
Princetown
50
Johanna

Curdies Inlet
(Inland)
MOUTH
Curdies Inlet
(Marine)
GREAT OCEAN RD
Irvine St
PETERBOROUGH
Newfield Bay
Imaginary line across the downstream side of the Great Ocean Road bridge at Peterborough.

2

Daniel Curdie

SCOTTISH-born settler **Dr Daniel Curdie** established his pastoral enterprise on a run of 19,000 acres, capable of supporting 2,340 cattle in 1840. Curdie had studied medicine in Edinburgh with the explorer David Livingstone. After arriving in Sydney at the age of 29 in 1839 Curdie decided grazing would be more lucrative than medicine and so he combined both. He travelled overland to Port Phillip with his nephew, Daniel Mackinnon, driving a mob of cattle. At one stage, they camped with their stock on what later became Melbourne's Botanical Gardens.

He established his homestead at *Tandarook*, an Aboriginal word for the "native bread" fungus, 18km south of the present town of Camperdown. A stone cross in Manifold Street, Camperdown, commemorates his endeavours.

The homestead was beside the river, which like the estuary was named after Curdie. He combined grazing with medicine, undertaking long journeys on horseback through the dingo-infested bush to tend his patients. According to the Shire of Hampden's records:

> Curdie had no trouble with the natives, who had great respect for the fearless way in which he travelled among them unarmed. The blacks looked on *Tandarook* as a place

of safety during tribal quarrels, and on one occasion, when almost an entire tribe was destroyed by a tribe from the Otway Ranges, the few whom escaped were cared for by the doctor. In return, they became self-appointed guardians of his holdings, and during his absence would challenge the approach of all who looked to them like unwelcome intruders. Curdie had great respect for native honesty. Although station stores stood out in the open in tarpaulin-covered drays with natives all around, nothing was ever pilfered, not even an ounce of sugar, which was their great temptation.

Curdie was an original member of the Hampden and Heytesbury District Roads Board and President of the Railway League, which was instrumental in having the railway line extended from Geelong to Warrnambool. He was the first President of the Shire of Hampden which extended from Skipton in the north to Peterborough and Port Campbell in the south. The Council met in Camperdown.

The colony of Victoria, with its government based in Melbourne, was established in 1851. At that time, those who had settled in the south-west of the state were largely isolated by the Otway Ranges. Road access from Geelong tracked north of the Ranges, through what are now the towns of Winchelsea, Colac, Camperdown and Terang to Warrnambool, Port Fairy and Portland.

Cobb and Co. began a coach service to Geelong from Warrnambool in 1866, three days a week. It left Warrnambool at 10pm arriving in Geelong next evening. The train to Spencer Street from Geelong would arrive at 10.45pm, a 24 hour journey. Most of the land to the east of Warrnambool was heavily forested and difficult to traverse through bogs and volcanic sink holes. The railway was extended to Camperdown in 1883, Terang in 1887 and Warrnambool in 1889. A line from Camperdown to Timboon, then known as the "Black Stump" was completed in April 1892.

Historian Rosamund Duruz outlined the challenges of living without roads in her work, *History of the Curdies River* (1976). She described the problems confronting Curdie in 1864 when some of his cattle went missing from his spring muster and were rumoured to have turned up at Glenample. In an attempt to recover them, Curdie had to ride around the south and west of the forest as far as the Hopkins River, then reverse eastwards along the cliffs before facing the return journey. Duruz recorded that one of his stockmen, C.J. Grayland Jr, who took part in the trek as a boy, told the tale when he was an old man:

> Next morning the homeward journey was commenced along the coast with 78 head of cattle. All went well until the present day Port Campbell racecourse (west of the Two Mile Bay road) and Peterborough were reached, when trouble was experienced getting them over water. A bar was on when the party went down, but had washed out before they went back. Two of the big bullocks made a desperate effort to escape and the stockman had a merry time watching the dogs capsize each beast in the sand. In bringing one of the runaways back it rushed into the mob, knocking several into the water, which solved the problem, for they swam across and were followed by the others. Jimmy, the black boy, who was assisting in driving, was knocked off his horse into the water and being unable to swim caught hold of one animal by the tail; the party thought he was drowned, but he came out on the other side, still holding the creature's tail. He had been struck on the calf of the leg and he was also sick from the amount of water he had swallowed, but his distress was greatly increased when he saw the blood. Dr Curdie and Mr Taubman attended to Jimmy while the rest of us held the cattle.

Two years later Curdie led a party of friends through the forest to Sherbrooke River to prove such a route was possible. His account of this trip "A Journey Through the Scrub – 1864" was published in *The Australasian* on 17 March 1864:

> We had a good native dog hunt; and by 2pm reached and crossed Curdies Inlet – not, however, without some ludicrous incidents. On entering on the sands of the bar, the two leading horses got into quicksand, out of which they got with difficulty. One of the gentlemen went on foot across, to get information from a resident where to cross safely. On crossing a small stream, two inches deep, of salt water coming over the bar from the sea, he met with a shoal of beautiful mullet, struggling to get from the lake into the sea. He forthwith began to throw them ashore, which others observing soon joined in the melee, when in ten minutes they caught 25 beautiful mullet, each three-quarters of a pound, which was the only pleasure we yet lacked. In half an hour they were in the pan, and we soon had as luxurious a fish dinner as an alderman could wish for.

Based on that experience, Curdie envisaged the opportunities for recreation and relaxation the area presented:

> A few hundred pounds might make the road such that a buggy could be driven five hours from Camperdown to Gellibrand. Then would be opened up to the health and pleasure seeking population 50 miles of sea coast, admirably adapted for villas, for sea-bathing, grounds for riding, second to none in the world; besides an endless variety of amusements in fishing, both by river and in the sea.

> As the climate is most salubrious for invalids, it is hoped that the Government will not allow this strip of country to be any longer unknown; by opening it up they will add to their revenue, and extend the available limits of the most desirable port of Victoria – our party having solved a problem said by many croakers to be impossible.

Despite Curdie's approach to nation building, Rosamund Duruz's research found that the constantly increasing flow of small selectors south of Camperdown and the surveying of Cobden in the middle of what had been his 'run' were at first a great annoyance to him:

> He was forced to buy much land and to erect expensive fences. In times he came to admire the hard work and tenacity of these people. He became the father figure of the whole district, public and private benefactor, sitting on Church and School Boards, chairing meetings and acting as Magistrate. Many famous visitors were entertained at Tanderook, including Mr Ellery, the government astronomer, and Baron von Mueller, creator and director of the Melbourne Botanic Gardens.
>
> As he grew old trouble overtook the doctor's family. In 1875 diphtheria struck his two youngest children, who died within twelve hours of each other. Another child on the estate was also a victim not long after an epidemic closed Curdie Vale school further down-stream …
>
> Fire in his big barn, outbreaks of pleura and scab among the animals and other family worries all helped to age Dr Curdie rapidly. When he died in 1884 the property was found to be insolvent. John, the second son, undertook to restore it to prosperity and in time all debts were paid off.

3

James Meek

JAMES MEEK, Peterborough's founding father, who was born in Great Yarmouth on the Norfolk coast, about 100 miles from Peterborough in England, had been an artist and prospector on the Ballarat goldfields. He had arrived in Sydney in 1838 and worked as a tutor to the children of Governor Gipps. In 1843, Meek married Julie Ann Craig, a governess who had arrived from England two years earlier. Living in Geelong, Meek described in his diary how he "followed my occupation as a fisherman till the outbreak of the Gold Diggings". Initially, the family lived in a tent in Ballarat. Meek recorded: "On 1ˢᵗ January 1852 I, with my tin dish, pick and shovel, met a man I had previously known, James Green ... We sank a fresh hole near to the junction of two creeks at the foot of Golden Point and bottomed on a splendid run of gold." Meek bought an allotment and built the first house in Ballarat for £406, a considerable sum.

Realising more money could be made in shopkeeping than prospecting, he set up a "Lemonade and Soda Factory" and store next to his home. His sketch of the properties is on display in the Sovereign Hill Museum, Ballarat, captioned "First House in Ballarat." He is regarded as a founder of Ballarat and is commemorated in the Ballarat City Chambers.

Years later, after giving up alcohol, Meek addressed a Temperance Meeting at Koroit. He revealed his Ballarat store had been a sly grog shop, the first in the town. The *Warrnambool Examiner* reported Meek's admission on Friday 4 May 1869, including his confession: "The Commissioners and the police used to call about and if the Police Commissioner wanted a five pound note he always knew where to come for it because he (Mr Meek) had to keep himself square."

As Meek's grandson James Dallimore wrote in the *Journal of the Meek Family History Fellowship,* Meek and his family made enough money in Ballarat to move to Port Melbourne in 1853, where Meek bought three fishing craft and a café. But their success was short-lived: "... a violent storm wrecked the boats at their moorings and then the café was destroyed by fire. Uninsured and deprived of all belongings, the family moved to Curdies Inlet."

There Meek built a hut. Dallimore records that Meek "obtained an old boat to find excellent fishing among the treacherous reefs, thus they became the first residents of what is now the township of Peterborough. The well he sunk, known as 'Meek's Well' served until it was filled in 120 years later. It was here he introduced fish curing and canning to Australia."

A reference in the *Warrnambool Examiner* of 9 February 1864 noted: "We have received smoked fish dried and cured at Curdies River by Mr Meek ... and have no hesitation in pronouncing them as equal to the herring and haddock of Yarmouth." He supplied centres as far afield as Ballarat and Melbourne.

In March that year, Meek formally applied at the Crown Lands Office in Melbourne for the land he was occupying and was disappointed to be told it was "swamp and scrub unfit for the purpose of agriculture". He knew otherwise, believing "better land I do not believe is to be found in the colony".

The family did not remain at Curdies Inlet for long. Finding living conditions unsuitable for a young family, the Meeks moved to Warrnambool. There James Meek set up as a fishmonger in premises on the corner of Banyan and Merri Streets and found excellent fishing in the locality. Later the family relocated to Melbourne, where Meek worked as librarian in the Melbourne Library.

John Dallimore noted that during his time in Melbourne, Meek produced a chart described in the Melbourne Library Index this way:

> Meek, James McKain, *Atlas of the Australian Colonies 1861, Meek's Historical and Descriptive Atlas of the British Colonies in Continental and Insular Australia* in which is given condensed history of each.

The work was exhibited at the International Exhibition in Melbourne in 1861. It received a First Class certificate from the Royal Commissioners and was thought to have earned a commendation from Queen Victoria, declaring him the best penman in the Australian colonies. As Dallimore notes:

> He was a very talented penman indeed, and produced many charts recording history, several of which survive in Victorian and New Zealand libraries and historic centres, for he spent some 16 years in New Zealand. He was also a writer and a poet but it is as an explorer and lecturer on natural resources that he made his greatest contribution to colonial development. He volunteered for the Burke and Wills Expedition without success and it was recognised by those who knew more of his abilities that had he been on that ill-fated venture there would have been no loss of life.

Meek and his family returned to Curdies Inlet in 1863, where they still had their hut and they lived either there or in Warrnambool for the next 11 years. As Elizabeth O'Callaghan detailed in *People*

Who Passed This Way, Meek supported his family with his fishing skills, fish canning business and pen and ink drawings.

At heart, however, Meek remained a prospector and the discovery of gold in the nearby Otway Ranges in 1856 had naturally aroused his interest. In July 1864, Meek, his son and John Fisher set off on a journey marred by days of torrential rain, swollen rivers and creeks, fallen timber, unchartered scrub, the heavy weight of their swags and a lame horse. A conscientious diarist, Meek later published his experiences in the *Examiner*. He recorded how, on 3 August, after digging two six-foot holes the previous day, they washed the gravel, slat and quartz for most of the day, finding specks of gold that increased in number from 10 to 51 to 170:

> All of us wet through, fatigued and went to bed, raining heavily, our bed clothes wet, in fact everything we had with us was fairly saturated. This night finished the last of our meat and the distance of 15 miles to walk to the station one of the most rugged countries desirable made us come to the conclusion to live on the flour and sugar we had with us rather than chance the journey and neglect our work.

And a couple of days later:

> Having had occasion to go down to the creek in the dark last evening I witnessed one of the most beautiful sights that ever was my lot to behold. Fisher was with me at the time. Standing under the dark foliage of a fern tree looking up the creek we observed hundreds of lights like those of diamonds and rubies emitting their sparkling lustre from the dark recess of its banks. These are what I believe are called glowworms. The sight was grand and baffles all description. (22 August 1864)

Meek concluded that the area probably had more promising quartz reefs containing gold in the vicinity. But the inaccessible terrain made commercial prospecting impractical.

By December 1864, however, he realised the Otways had little more to offer than "fool's gold" after another exploratory trip with C.F. Wilkinson, a rock expert from the Victorian Geological Survey Department. Together they retraced Meek's footsteps from his earlier visit and located the areas from which he had taken samples that had appeared promising. But writing in the *Examiner* on 13 December 1864 Meek explained:

> Mr Wilkinson carefully examined the stuff and pronounced it to be of the same kind in appearance as that from whence the gold is taken from on the general diggings of the colony, and would deceive any practical digger as to its gold producing qualities, unless thoroughly versed in the science of geology. We then proceeded farther up the creek, Mr W. noticing every particular stone in its bed, and finding carboniferous in large detached pieces. I then took Mr W. farther on and showed him a section in the bank of the creek on the south side, which I had previously taken to be a sort of slate rock, greatly resembling in appearance the slaty country in the Mt. Alexander district, and from which so much gold has been taken, Mr W. at once pronounced it to be the carboniferous sandstone rock cropping out, and was fully satisfied that the whole of the Cape Otway Ranges consisted of the same kind of formation, and that no paying goldfield will ever be found in its locality.

Meek's command of English and his appreciation of his surroundings were evident in his description of his survey of Curdies Inlet, published in a *Warrnambool Examiner* supplement of 1 July 1864, headed "Description of Curdies Inlet As surveyed by J.M. Meek and Son 17 April 1864":

> Curdies Inlet is situated about 30 miles to the eastward of the seaport town of Warrnambool and about 17 miles west of the river Gellibrand; its entrance to the sea lies about

north east and south west. The present outlet to the sea is obstructed by a number of calcareous rocks, a portion of which at one time no doubt formed the headland of the western side of its now shallow lake. That it has been a harbour of some magnitude there is sufficient evidence to prove, for by standing on an eminence of its western side, the observer can readily discern its original course and looking east can trace it along the seashore of a distance of nearly a mile, a number of sand hummocks, which owe their accumulation to prevailing wind, at the end of which stands out in bold relief the headland of the former eastern entrance. In its present state it is very seldom that a boat can with safety be brought into its waters, owing to the heavy surf breaking at all times on its outlet.

About 300 yards distant from the sea, a deep channel is met with, its width about 100 feet and containing an average depth of water from 14 to 18 feet at low tide; it continues for a distance of about three quarters of a mile, when it abruptly terminates in a very shallow mud flat, at very low tide not containing sufficiency of water to admit the passage of a boat. On either side of the channel, before arriving at the flats, are the remains of immense oyster beds, many square acres of the flats being wholly occupied by decayed oyster shells.

Meeks's surveys and descriptions of the district inspired others to settle there, including farming pioneers James and Jessie MacGillivray. Meek was also the major contributing factor in prompting the surveying of the townships of Peterborough and Princetown.

As Bonnie MacKenzie revealed in her book *My Grandmother's Story*:

Jessie was well acquainted with the name James McKain Archibald Meek and, with good reason, considered him

the founder of Peterborough. Years before there was any
settlement in this coastal region he sailed his yacht into the
mouth of the river and sunk a well from which Jessie many
years later had dipped fresh water.

In February 1865 Meek embarked on an historic journey,
accompanied by Dr James, George Foote and James Williams.
They were to explore the mouth of the Curdies River to Terang.
In doing so, they pioneered the route that is today Ayrford Road.
Elizabeth O'Callaghan noted that Meek kept a diary of the two
week trip. Extracts were published in the *Examiner* later that year.
Much of the journey was tough:

> I went ahead cutting the scrub during the time the doctor
> was boiling our billy. On my return I felt a severe pain
> in my right eye: I asked the doctor to look at it but he
> could perceive nothing: the pain became intense and I
> again asked him to see if anything had got into it. He then
> discovered that a leech had made fast to the ball of my eye;
> after several efforts to remove it, he at last succeeded; the
> consequence was that my eye was full of blood and I lost
> my sight for some time.

The following year, 1866, the Parish of Narrawaturk was established and land on the western side of the river, including Meek's
hut was marked on a survey map for a township. By then, the township had been surveyed by Nathan Thornley, 94 lots marked out
and the township named Peterborough. Meek bought one of the
first lots for his son.

Sadly, the last of more than 100 references to James Meek in the
Warrnambool Examiner from 1855 to November 1869 was news
of his insolvency. The cause of the problem, the paper reported,
was "heavy expenses attending the compiling of a book on the
resources of the Western District from inability to obtain money
due to him from work done in collecting agricultural statistics and

clerical services rendered to the Crown and from present want of employment". It was reported James McKain Meek of Curdies Inlet, artist, owed liabilities of £1001.13s 9d with assets of only £271 and one pence, a "deficiency" of £821 13s 8d (12 November 1869).

In 1874 Meek and his family (except one daughter, Marianne, who had married Peter Dallimore and was living near Lake Gillear) went to New Zealand. There they stayed for 16 years, with Meek exploring the countryside and producing his calligraphy. He returned to Australia in 1890, when he found "the land which in the 1860s was only occupied by the kangaroo and a few natives was now a thriving district with the township of Port Campbell" (O'Callaghan). He indicated that he had explored the country for the benefit of those occupying it in 1890. He returned to Ballarat, working as an assistant bookkeeper and producing his pen and ink drawings. He died in 1899, aged 84 and was buried in the Warrnambool Cemetery. His grave carries a plaque commissioned by the Ballarat Historical Society, acknowledging his part in history. As Elizabeth O'Callaghan observed:

> James McKain Meek looms large in our local history as a man of vision, energy and talent, lacking, perhaps a keen business brain but accepting with some considerable measure of resourcefulness, the setbacks in his life and always ready to take on new challenges.

4

Jemima Vans Robertson

JEMIMA Robertson (née Wallace-Dunlop) arrived in the Mt Shadwell/Ellerslie district, north east of Warrnambool in 1853. She was born in Ayrshire, Scotland, in 1800 and came from minor Scottish nobility. She was the daughter of Lieutenant John Wallace-Dunlop of the 89th Foot Regiment, Scotland, and his second cousin Magdalene Dunlop. Robertson was a granddaughter of Sir John Dunlop and Frances Anna Wallace, who was the daughter of Sir Thomas Wallace, 5th Baron of Craigie and Lochryan in Scotland. Jemima and her sister, Flora Rachel Wallace-Dunlop, were among the youngest of a large family of at least 11. Their father died in Neemuch, India, in 1834 while serving with the 46th Native Infantry.

Jemima married her cousin, Lieutenant-Colonel Henry Dundas Robertson, on 31 January 1828 in Mumbai (Bombay). Henry was a Lieutenant Colonel in the 21st Native Infantry of the HEIC (Honourable East India Company) and also served as the magistrate and collector in Poonah before dying of cholera in 1845 aged 55. He was highly respected by the local population. At that point, the East India Company ruled large areas of India, with its own private armies exercising military power and administrative functions, a system that prevailed until after the Indian Mutiny in 1857 when the British Government took control. Henry's brother, Major General

Archibald Robertson, was a director of the Honourable East India Company.

According to Jemima's death certificate she had had ten children with only two surviving. Her surviving son, Henry Dundas Robertson, was born in 1829 at Ootacamund in southern India and her surviving daughter, Catherine Flora Robertson, was born in 1830 at Ahmednuggur, Poona. According to family legend Jemima had an Rh negative blood group, which may have accounted for the deaths of so many of her children.

Possibly Jemima Robertson was encouraged to emigrate to Australia by her sister Flora Wallace-Dunlop, who had arrived here in 1849 with her husband Alexander Cunynghame Faerlie Wallace–Dunlop. By 1850 they had bought the station property *Parasia* from Captain William Adam and renamed it *Hexham Park.* Jemima had arrived in the Mount Shadwell district by 1853 and Flora had been widowed the previous year. Jemima's son Henry Dundas Robertson, 23, arrived in Sydney from Manila on board the *Helen Baird* in July 1852.

Jemima made her first investment in Australia in 1853 when she bought the lease on *Kona Warren* near Mortlake, the Aboriginal for "home of the black swan" (later renamed *Connewarren/ Woolongoon*), covering about 18,132 acres, from George Rodger. In 1851 Jemima's nephew Anthony Mackenzie-Ross, aged 19, came to the colony (later dropping the Ross from the family name) and worked for Jemima at *Kona Warren*. He later managed the property for her. Anthony was the son of Jemima and Flora's sister, Susan Agnes Elanora Wallace-Dunlop.

The lease of the land at *Kona Warren* would have been cancelled in the late 1850s, but on 25 April 1860, at a sale in Warrnambool, Jemima purchased the property from the Crown for £1 per acre, much of it in the name of her son Henry Dundas Robertson. She also bought land in the name of Charles Robertson. Jemima continued to live in the *Kona Warren* homestead but gave her nephew Anthony MacKenzie £800 to build himself a bluestone house, which then became the main homestead. In 1865 Anthony married Grace Beveridge Murdoch.

Despite her wealth, Jemima was thrifty. She once ordered wallpaper samples from England and when the supplier wrote months later asking if she was going to place an order she wrote back explaining she had been able to do all the papering required with the sample and did not need any more. In 1870, Jemima divided her land into two parts. She remained on *Kona Warren* homestead with 640 acres and leased 17,492 acres to Anthony MacKenzie. The leased portion and the new homestead became *Woolongoon*. Jemima had settled into the life of the community and by 1870, when a meeting at Ellerslie (then known as Letts Ford) decided to proceed with the building of a Presbyterian church, Jemima donated two acres of land, with an extra acre reserved for a manse. She remained a generous and constant patron of the church.

Jemima laid the foundation stone for the Ellerslie church on Tuesday, 1 November (All Saints Day) in 1870. In his address to the gathering, the Rev Robert Sutherland said:

> You are known to them (the community) as one of the oldest colonists in the district. They all respect your high character, great energy, and large benefice. You are a large contributor to all benevolent purposes, and from the very foundation of the colony, you have been one of the most generous supporters of our church, and this church at Ellerslie, owes its erection principally to your munificence. I have therefore much pleasure in asking you to lay the foundation stone.

The church was completed the following year and in 1872 Jemima gave money to provide a bell and a collection of 100 children's books for the Sunday school. She also gave a fine bookcase, made by a local Aborigine from the *Connewarren* estate.

Jemima spent a good deal of her later life at Peterborough. By 1874 she had obtained the title to an allotment on the corner of Blair and Robertson Streets where she built her seaside home, which the locals called *The Big House*. Years later, it was to become *Blair Athol* guest house. She obtained the property through the default of a stock agent in Warrnambool who had gone broke owing her money. The title was in part settlement of his debt.

Jemima later bought 18 more lots of nine acres in the township of Peterborough between 1876 and 1882, two years before her death. She also bought five acres north of what is now Halladale Road; three half-acre lots on the corner of Irvine Road and Hamilton Streets which she donated to the Presbyterian Church; 49 acres (Crown Allotment 106) on the western side of the Old Peterborough-Warrnambool Road which she also gave to the Presbyterian Church; and 710 acres on the west and north sides of the Old Peterborough-Warrnambool Road. Being a woman in her 80s did not limit her ability to acquire yet more properties.

In 1882 at Mortlake, two years before Jemima died, her long time manager and nephew Anthony MacKenzie died of pneumonia

The Big House, later Blair Athol guest house, built 1875

at the age of 52. Anthony was buried in the Hexham cemetery. His widow Grace and their eight children continued to live in the *Woolongoon* homestead. Grace lived on until 1919.

In his memoirs, *The Weatherlys of Woolongoon*, William Weatherly cast a light on the personality of the formidable Jemima:

> Mrs Robertson was I believe a strong character. In my youth, John Graham (senior) was manager at *Woolongoon*. He had been overseer at the time when my grandfather bought it. He remembered Mrs Robertson well. His son was overseer when I took over in 1944 and had stories to tell about the old lady which no doubt he was told by his father. The only one I remember is unprintable.

Jemima Vans Robertson died on 13 October 1884 at the age of 84 and her death was registered at Hexham. As per her will, she was buried in the Ellerslie churchyard. The executors of her estate were Daniel Mackinnon on *Maridayallock* and William Armstrong of *Hexham Park*. Jemima's funeral was described locally as a grand affair with a two-horse hearse and attendants to *Connewarren Station* (32 miles) and on to Ellerslie Presbyterian Church enclosure. Eighteen black crepe hand bands were provided at five shillings each and the total funeral expenses were £29/10s. A costly stone was brought from England to mark the spot where her remains were interred.

The *Warrnambool Standard's* obituary of 14 October 1884 reported:

> The deceased lady had been a resident of the district from the early days of settlement, and was well and widely known throughout this part of the colony. She owned the *Connewarren* and *Woolongoon* estates, the latter which was rented by the nephew the late Anthony MacKenzie.

The deceased enjoyed a long lease of life, being in her 85th year at the time of her death, and was remarkable for the mental and physical vigour she displayed even in her latest years.

At the time of her death, Jemima was the largest property owner in the township of Peterborough and still owned *The Big House* which was probably the second house built in the surveyed area. She had consolidated her lots of the township land into one, covering almost half the township area.

She had lost eight babies in India all those decades ago and her surviving son, Henry, had died in India 17 years earlier. Her daughter Catherine was living in New Zealand as, presumably were Catherine's eight surviving children. Only two of Henry's children had survived. Alexander was in England, and Jemima's grand-daughter, the recently married Teenyah, Countess Zichy-Woinarski, was living in Ballarat. She was the only member of Jemima's family in Victoria, if not Australia. A week after Jemima's death Teenyah would name her new-born daughter Alexandrina Vans in honour of the child's great-grandmother, Jemima Vans Robertson.

When Jemima's will was probated in March 1885 her estate was worth £106,364 which today would be valued at about $13 million. Her executors ran her estate until her grandson, Alexander Dundas Robertson, arrived in 1889. He was reputed to have left huge debts behind him in England. Alexander, born in India, had been sent to England for his education in 1881 aged 15 and had been living with a school master at Rugby. He was a young man in his early 20s when he inherited his grandmother's wealth.

Alexander was to live in extravagant style at *Woolongoon* where he built a houseboat on Lake Connewarren. In 1893 at Sedberg in Yorkshire he married Evelyn Hilda Upton-Cottrell–Dormer, a descendent of an aristocratic Oxford family. His time at *Connewarren* and *Woolongoon* had been brief. Like many Victorians, the 1892 depression cost him dearly, with the Bank of Australiasia selling up his properties. *The Big House* at Peterborough was bought by Helen Blair in 1892 and the title to the 700 acre farm at Peterborough was transferred to the Bank of Australasia in 1895. The following year James Arthur Robilliard, who had been leasing it, bought it from the Bank. In all he farmed it for about 25 years. James Robilliard, a prominent Peterborough resident, came from the Isle of Jersey. He married Helen Beckett in 1879

Thomas Asche

and they had 10 children, including three sons who farmed in the district.

The sale of *Woolongoon,* to William Weatherly of Halifax Street, Brighton for £46,596, 12 shillings (£2 pounds, 1 shilling per acre) had been completed on 5 April 1895. It included the parishes of Yeth Youang and Ellerslie. Alexander had mortgaged it to the Bank of Australasia the previous year.

After leaving the Mortlake district in the early 1890s Alexander travelled to the Transvaal, which later became part of South Africa, where he died in 1915.

A contemporary of Jemima Robertson who was also an early land buyer in Peterborough was **Thomas Asche** (1826-1898) who bought Allotment 3, Section 1 at the Peterborough land sale in Warrnambool in 1866.

According to Margaret Kiddle in *Men of Yesterday* (MUP 1963), Asche was "one of the most notorious speculators in Victoria … a burly golden bearded Norwegian, with a bone breaking hand clasp". A qualified lawyer, he came to Victoria as a gold digger and later earned his living as a storekeeper and mounted policeman. Kiddle recounted:

> His fondness for whisky was never known to cloud his prematurely sharp judgment. 'Tom the Boy' looked and was a Viking adventurer, best avoided by those who wanted to play the land market. Gambling was his life, but he gambled to win and cared nothing for those who lost.
>
> Asche was known in mining camps and at land sales throughout the whole Western District, but especially round Camperdown which he made the centre of his operations. The occupation of all sharks whether working for themselves or for a super-shark such as Asche was to act as agents for squatters. As soon as it was known that certain sections of land were to be thrown open to selection, the sharks gathered to investigate the situation. When the selection took place they knew exactly who wanted the land, whether squatter or potential selector. They approached whoever could pay the most (inevitably the squatter) and asked for commission on every acre of land which could be secured.
>
> Asche, unable to resist from speculative enterprise continued to flourish until he was swept to ruin in the economic debacle of the nineties.

He became a Geelong town councillor in 1870 and acquired Mack's Hotel in 1871. In 1876 he moved to the Union Club Hotel in Melbourne, and 10 years later to the Royal Hotel, Sydney. After heavy losses in 1893 he sold the Royal, but from 1896 ran the Imperial Hotel, Wynyard Square, where he died in 1898.

5

James Irvine and his dynasty

JAMES IRVINE is a name synonymous with Peterborough, and the man who made it so was actually James Irvine 2nd, who arrived in Australia in 1865 from Enniskillen, Northern Ireland, at the age of 17. He arrived with his father James Irvine 1st, who had been a school teacher, his mother Annabella and four of his 13 siblings. James 1st found work as a overseer at Thomas Shaw's *Wooriwyrite* and at *Hexham Park* homestead, near Mortlake in Western Victoria. In his history of Warrnambool Shire called *Of Many Things*, C.E. Sayers recorded that James 1st's grandson, James Irvine 3rd talked in later years of his grandfather building haystacks for squatters and working as a stock overseer on sheep runs. James 2nd also worked at *Hexham*.

Jenny Porteous, the great-great granddaughter of James Irvine 1st says: "James Irvine 2nd (1848-1919) was in demand as the leader

Hexham Park homestead

of the hunting, shooting and fishing parties because of his pleasant personality and organisational skills." James 2nd married at Hexham Park and had two sons, James 3rd, George, known as Jim, and John who died aged 22 in 1910.

Former Peterborough resident Ruth Grimwade recalled Jim telling her how

> … he used to walk to school in Hexham and was always frightened when he had to cross a paddock where the bullocks regularly chased him. One day Mr Armstrong (the owner of *Hexham Park*) offered Jim sixpence to go round the property with him in the buggy and open the gates. When they came to the fateful paddock, Jim confessed that he always dreaded being chased by the bullocks. Soon afterwards Mr Armstrong presented Jim with a little Shetland mare, and said "Here you are boy, now you can ride to school and the bullocks won't hurt you." Later, when the Irvines moved to Peterborough, Jim took the mare with him, and broke two of her foals into harness, and used to drive visitors around with them in a tiny buggy known as the Bambi cart.

Shire of Warrnambool records show the Irvine family began leasing land as part of the Bay of Islands Farm at Peterborough shortly after arriving in Australia. The holding included a house with 174 acres and another block of 58 acres. Another entry shows William Irvine (another son of James 1st) leasing 253 acres nearby.

According to official land records, the site on the north east corner of what is now Irvine and Mac's Streets was initially bought by William Hamilton of Mortlake for £7 in August 1866. Thomas Shaw bought it in 1873, and *Peterborough House* was built on the site as a guesthouse in about 1887, with several partners, including Thomas Shaw and James Irvine 2nd, who moved in with his family as manager. By that stage, his two brothers, William and Gerard, were running the Bay of Islands farms. But James 2nd had found his calling as well. The guesthouse was a success and he built it from strength to strength. James 2nd had the title registered in his name in 1891, transferred from Thomas Shaw.

Irvine advertised in the *Warrnambool Standard* in February 1886, offering rooms at "moderate charges":

> Visitors can obtain good fishing in the River and sea. Splendid sea bathing, three minutes' walk from the House. Good shooting, kangaroo hunting, etc, etc … Good meals and beds. Good paddocks for horses and perfectly secure. Also a boat kept on the river for the use of visitors.

Ruth Grimwade noted that hotel guests

> … all made comments about the wonderful fishing and shooting obtainable, and also the hospitality dispensed by Mr and Mrs Irvine. The boarding house was simple and somewhat primitive, but there were always roaring log fires, and good food cooked by Mrs Irvine. One of the visitors particularly mentioned his enjoyment of driving the little horses and buggy …

On a walking trip from Warrnambool in 1887, Captain A.S. Brown wrote:

> The walk was so pleasant that it seemed very short, and at 1 o'clock I found myself at Peterborough, or as it is better known Curdies Inlet. Here I found a very nice house kept by Mr James Irvine for the convenience of the travelling public. Here I resolved to stop for the night with the view to looking about me the next day. Mr Irvine informed me that in the summer large numbers of visitors come to Peterborough. He himself last summer accommodated 200, attracted there by the sport that is to be got with rod and gun, and by the natural surroundings of the place. At the present time the mouth of the river is silted up causing the water to overflow its natural low lying banks, which gives it the

appearance of it being about half a mile broad at this place. When the flood waters come down they will find their way out to sea and the river will be confined to its natural course again. The punt, which at the time of my visit was lying idle on the bank, will then be brought into use for the conveying of passengers. Mr Irvine has a very good boat for the use of his visitors which, when the weather is favourable, he sails in the bay where very good fishing is obtained.

In 1903 Peterborough House became the *Peterborough Hotel* and after his death in 1919 it transferred to his widow, Ester Irvine, and his son, James George Irvine (James 3rd), who had been born in 1879. James 3rd had two sons, James M. Irvine (James 4th – called Bill Irvine) and John Stewart Irvine (also known as Jack).

The only other house in Peterborough when the Irvine family first arrived in Peterborough had been built by Rev William Hamilton of Mortlake, where he used to take his family on holidays. He had bought the land on the corner of what is now Irvine and Mac's Street (the opposite corner to the boarding house) and the home was known as "Hamilton Cottage". The title to this block was registered in the name of Margaret Hamilton in 1875. James Irvine later acquired that property and it became an annex to his boarding house. He added a sitting room and extra bedrooms. "The Cottage" still has part of the early shingle roof lining the verandah today.

In the early 1900s, the *Peterborough Hotel* was advertised as: "Superior accommodation, 80 rooms, sewered & electric light, good golf course, pro kept, excellent sea and river fishing, bathing, open sea and pool – Jas Irvine Prop". Bonnie MacKenzie recalled the "delightful little golf links , with styles over fences and the box thorn hedges and swamps forming natural hazards, had been taking shape and golf was an attraction." The Hotel was destroyed by fire in 1965, but "The Cottage" remained.

Because there was no bridge over the river, the Irvines used to drive an enormous drag, pulled by four horses, to meet guests from the train at Timboon and they would be rowed across the river to reach the guesthouse. It was a sign of the hotel's popularity and success that by 1905, James Irvine 2nd provided a "regular service" for the hotel using nine horses and three coaches with capacity for 22 passengers. During holidays, the service was increased to include 14 horses, five coaches and a capacity for 34 passengers.

Sadly, James Irvine 2nd was drowned crossing that river in June 1919. He was swept away when attempting a crossing he had done many times before. He had been attending a funeral at Port Campbell and his wife had been watching out for him to come home for hours. Despite this tragedy and agitation by the Port Campbell Progress Association, it was to be a further eight years before a bridge was built over the Curdies River. A monument in the form of a stone wall of rough cast granite with metal spike on top facing the ocean at Paddy's Point honours James Irvine's memory.

Following his father's death, Jim Irvine (3rd) ran the business. Ruth Grimwade recalled Jim as a "wonderful character" who would "drive us for wonderful picnics to the Loch Ard Gorge and the Strawberry Gardens near Port Campbell, grilling chops over an open fire for our lunch, as it was an all day trip over the unspeakable corduroy roads."

He was also a farmer. As neither William nor Gerard Irvine, brothers of James 2nd, had children, the original farm of James 1st eventually passed to Jim and he increased the holding, after his father, James 2nd had bought *The Lodge* block of 450 acres from James Robilliard in 1909. *The Lodge* farm was originally part of Jemima Robertson's property on the Peterborough-Warrnambool Road extending to the Curdies River Estuary.

The original farm of James 1st was later passed to and farmed by Bill Irvine while "The Lodge Farm" was passed to and farmed by John Irvine. Bill Irvine was a Councillor in Warrnambool for many years and Chairman of the Foreshore Reserve Committee. John was instrumental in reviving the Golf Club after 1958.

Tom MacKenzie's coaches outside Peterborough Hotel, 1905

Peterborough Hotel, 1906, the coach ready for departure to the Timboon railway station

James Irvine's mail coach outside Peterborough house. The driver James Delaney was on the box 1915-1925

Peterborough from the air, 1919

Approach and putting competition, Peterborough Hotel, 1919

Bridge 1927 with Jessie MacGillivray driving the first pile

Bridge under construction. Opened by James George Irvine,
3 December 1927

Bridge nearly completed, 1927, with Jessie MacGillivray at left

The Armstrongs setting off for an outing

Roy de Crespigney, Bill Irvine, unknown, Jim Irvine, February 1951

6

The Macs and their legacy
Charles and Jessie MacGillivray

UNLIKE most of the Peterborough district's pioneers who had immigrated to Australia from the British Isles, Charles and Janet (Jessie) MacGillivray and their two small children, who established their home, *Oak Bank*, on the eastern bank of Curdies Inlet in 1873, were first generation Australians. Two years earlier, inspired by James Meek's published descriptions of the areas, Charles MacGillivray had come to the area seeking suitable land for farming. He has heard a great deal about the area and made up his mind as soon as he saw it. He rode straight back to the family property *Skye Hill* at Purnim, about 20km north east of Warrnambool, and set about buying land. The fact their story, and that of their descendants, can be told in such detail is due to the talent and skill of Jessie MacKenzie, who wrote down much of the family history in diaries and a book and their grand-daughter, Ann Wilkinson, who summarised and updated the material in 2003. It is on their work that this chapter, most of the next two and parts of the Shipwreck chapter, are based.

MacGillivray and his brother-in-law had built a small dwelling and roofed it with bark shingles from the Great Southern Forest (later known as Heytesbury). With courage and practicality, underpinned by a deep Christian faith, Jessie set about making

Charles MacGillivray (front centre) with friends

the primitive little house a home. In the early months, without a chimney in the house, she cooked outside over an open fire. She also gave birth to a daughter, named Margaret Euphemia but within the family and to her friends she was always Effie or Eff. Charles and Jessie were to have three more children, all born *at Oak Bank*. Sarah (Sadie) Adeline was born in 1876, Mary (Molly) Isabella in 1879 and John Alexander Valentine (Val) in 1883. Sadly, they lost their two eldest children, Jessie and Archie, in the diphtheria epidemic of 1887. Val drowned in the well at *Oak Bank* in 1891. Despite the fact the well was surrounded by a high paling fence, with a securely latched gate, Val and his playmate managed to gain entry. He was found by his mother and her father, Andrew Macdonald.

Charles's brother Duncan also came to the area in 1973, living in a nearby cottage. Their nearest neighbour, no more than a quarter mile away was C.S. Affleck who had bought a small portion of the Buckley's Creek run and also selected adjoining coastal land to the east.

In the early years, Charles MacGillivray was often away shearing for months in the summer. Later he worked as contractor for the local Shire, building roads and bridges locally, which kept him closer to home. A cutting in Timboon that bore his name for many years is now known as Heywood's Road.

As the years passed *Oak Bank* became a productive farm. They were busy, productive years in which Charles, Duncan and others were preoccupied with clearing, building and fencing, using palings and logs cut from forest timber. From the hay loft above the stables, the view stretched for miles over forest and sea. According to her family, it was from there, in 1908, that Jessie MacGillivray, using her telescope, was able to observe the salvage efforts and the final destruction of the *Falls of Halladale* across the estuary. She chronicled her observations carefully.

Oak Bank was good country, well drained with friable black soil. Charles established a piggery and built a smokehouse where he cured excellent bacon. They ran cattle and sheep and Jessie kept hens. The river flats grew large crops of potatoes. On a warm north wall she trained a grape vine and they had an extensive orchard in which grew several varieties of apple trees. Oats were grown, hay was stored and the yard was paved with huge stones brought from the beach nearby. A separate small dairy with two bails was also built for Jessie who kept a herd of Jersey cows all her active life. Captain Robilliard gave her a Jersey bull calf which he had brought especially for her from the Channel Island as a gift of appreciation for her kindness and hospitality to his wife and family during his many long absences at sea.

The family wasted nothing. What was not needed for the household went to the pigs. Initially their intent was simply to be self-supporting as there was no way of getting excess produce to market. This was soon to change, however. In April 1878 (shortly before the wreck of the *Loch Ard*) the lighter ship *Asia* called at Port Campbell (which had been settled by a few families in 1865) with merchandise from Warrnambool and took away a cargo of farm produce. While the fine weather continued the vessel made further trips and in 1879 work began building a jetty. It was completed in 1880. When the trading ketch *Hannah Thompson* began calling on a regular basis at Port Campbell it became possible to market the district's produce regularly. Charles MacGillivray secured from Hamilton Bros, the sons of the Rev William Hamilton of Mortlake, a lease with the option to purchase the Delburg Estate property at Port Campbell.

In 1879, the Blair family came to live just north of *Oak Bank* and young Mrs Blair and Jessie MacGillivray became friends. Eventually, the Blairs were also to play a large part in Peterborough after they bought *The Big House* in Helen Blair's name in 1892 and

Peterborough Post Office, 1896, with Effie MacGillivray (left),
James Pippad, unnamed, and Jessie MacGillivray (doorway)

she and Robert Blair moved their family into Peterborough. They
enlarged *The Big House* and renamed it *Blair Athol* and opened a
guest house. Robert Blair bought a nearby farm which he managed
while Helen concentrated on the guest house.

Initially, the MacGillivray children received a good educational
grounding at home but eventually the three eldest were sent to board
for a time. On Monday, 16 March 1885, State School No 2650
Wallaby Hill, "the grass-tree school", was opened. All the pupils
had a long walk. If the MacGillivray children took the shorter track
through the bush, it was still almost three miles and they had to
cross the Squirrel and Wallaby Creeks over fallen logs. Walking
to school in winter was a misery, with rain, mud and leeches. For
those coming from the west bank it also meant a dangerous crossing
over the river. In 1889 little Henry Croft was drowned on his way
to school and finally the Education Department agreed a school in
Peterborough itself was needed. School No 3024 was opened in
the first wooden Presbyterian church which the MacGillivrays had

been instrumental in building in 1885. It was closed in April 1893. Wallaby Hill School closed in 1894 and formal education again lapsed.

In 1893 the MacGillivray girls – Effie, Sadie and Molly – had reared 40 orphan lambs and when they were sold their father said they could buy whatever they wished with the money. They decided upon a piano. Their friend Miss Emery, governess to the Touton children, taught the girls to play. The piano brought great happiness to *Oak Bank*, still shadowed by Val's death. It had always been a hospitable home, but it now became the centre of many happy social occasions. All of the young people in the district were good riders and in their free time would ride long distances for the entertainment they organised themselves – cricket matches, boating and fishing excursions in summer and dances, concerts and musical and card (mainly cribbage) evenings in the colder months.

Many of the social evenings were held at *Oak Bank*. Tom McKenzie, the youngest of the 13 children of Newfield pioneers John and Elizabeth (Betsy) MacKenzie, had known the MacGillivrays since 1875 and was one of those who gathered regularly around the new piano. Sometimes he brought his violin (which is still in the family) and accompanied the piano while Miss Effie MacGillivray sang. She had a fine voice and her favourite piece was reportedly "An Arab's Farewell to His Steed". As her daughter Aileen said years later, her mother was "really quite remarkable ... she could shear a sheep as well as any man and ride and shoot and fish".

Thomas Ingles McKenzie and Margaret Euphemia MacGillivray were married at Wendouree, near Ballarat on 28 March 1900. Initially, they lived with Tom's widowed mother at Inglewood and had two children, Keith Inglis in 1901 and Aileen (Aila) in 1903. In 1904 they settled in Peterborough.

In 1910, Charles MacGillivray and Tom McKenzie bought 259

acres on the west side of the Peterborough Warrnambool Road from James Robilliard.

Charles MacGillivray died in 1915. Extracts from a local newspaper at the time of his death captured his life and times:

> The late gentleman … like many of the old pioneers his memory was richly stored with happenings connected with the early struggles of men and women who went into almost inaccessible corners of our continent and scorning to ask assistance of the government, hewed out a home for themselves and their families by indomitable energy … He saw the rise of the township from the fisherman's huts … to the present fashionable watering place with its hundreds of golfers and fishing enthusiasts.

7

The MacKenzies

A photograph of Peterborough taken in 1906 shows only four houses: *Peterborough House* (the hotel), Hamilton's Cottage across the road from it, *Sunny Brae* (the Post office) towards the northern end of Mac's Street and *The Big House* (*Blair Athol*) on the corner of Blair and Robertson Streets.

The MacKenzie family moved to Hamilton's Cottage. The building, which James Irvine later bought and enlarged (and which was later owned for many years by Mr and Mrs Desmond Moore) still stands.

Backed by his father-in-law, Charles MacGillivray, Tom established a coaching business. He secured the Peterborough/ Timboon mail contract and his coach and two buggies were rarely idle. Despite its isolation, Peterborough was becoming well known for holidaying and the MacKenzie coach took sightseers to the best spots along the coast, with Loch Ard Gorge and London Bridge being popular destinations for picnics.

Tom MacKenzie was an expert horseman and bred his own horses, which he broke to harness and saddle. When they were young the five MacKenzie children each had their own ponies. Tom MacKenzie acquired land in Peterborough for a house and stables (the stables were accessed from what is now Schomberg

Road) and rented grazing land to the west of Peterborough, which he later bought. He also leased 400 acres of coastal frontage from the government and ran cattle and sheep as well as his horses.

In April 1907, the MacKenzie's third child Betsy was born at Warrnambool. Later that year Sarah (Sadie) MacGillivray, the popular Post Mistress at Peterborough for nine years, married Robert Milne of Mepunga. The reception was held in a large marquee in the garden at *Oak Bank*. Mary (Molly) MacGillivray became the new Post Mistress. In late 1908, Tom and Effie MacKenzie had a small house built up the hill from Hamilton's Cottage. The family moved in and named their new home *Tulach Ard*. Whenever Effie had money to spare the home was enlarged. By the time the family opened a guest house in about 1911, *Tulach Ard* was large and rambling, with a long north-facing verandah. The family also built a cottage alongside. Eventually this was enlarged to contain the General Store and Post Office. Tom and Effie MacKenzie's fourth baby, Jean (Bon to her family and friends)

Tulach Ard, 1908

was born in December 1908. Their last child, Ian MacGillivray McKenzie was born at Nurse Yates' private Hospital at Camperdown in February 1911. Nurse Agnes Yates was Tom MacKenzie's sister and a noted midwife.

In 1915/16, Miss Ruth Tregea, who was shortly to become Mrs Jim Blair, undertook to teach Peterborough children. The Education Department supplied desks for what was known as a "subsidised school". There were never any more than seven children at a time attending, including Aileen and Bet MacKenzie. Aila MacKenzie later recalled the daily challenge of out-running the hotel geese on the way to school. The creatures gathered regularly around the large swamp in the middle of the town and would pursue any children cutting across 'their' paddock. The Irvine children, who had a governess, Mrs Seaton, did not attend this school. Mrs Seaton taught piano to the MacKenzie girls and the Irvines. She and Effie MacKenzie were good friends, except at the bridge table, where they were fiercely competitive.

The holiday period, though short, was important to Peterborough. It brought in ready money, and while the farming community surrounding it was not greatly impacted by the visitors, tourism provided their sons and daughters with seasonal work, releasing them briefly from the isolation of the farms. *Tulach Ard*'s register reflected the change in times in the 1920s and 1930s. Many of the guests came from further afield, many travelling down by car. By today's standards the guest house facilities were basic but comfortable and relaxing, and visitors returned year after year. Like all hostesses of the era, Effie MacKenzie took pride in laying a "fine table" in her dining room that could seat at least 30. Fishing was her lifelong love and she knew all the best spots and regularly took guests out on her own boat. Under the pseudonym "Sea Foam" she wrote a weekly segment on Peterborough happenings for the local newspaper. She, like her mother, kept a diary and was a prolific letter writer.

Ken and Aileen Row's post office and store, c. 1950

About 1924 the original wooden Presbyterian church was sold (not without protest) for removal. It had served the community well and many missionaries and ministers who preached in it were to become famous. One of these was the Rev John Flynn, founder of the Royal Flying Doctor Service.

After heated debate, which saw the older members of the congregation outvoted, the decision was made to break Jemima Robertson's Deed of Gift by selling much of the land she had left to the church. Tom MacKenzie, who was one of those who did not think the decision ethical, said after the meeting, "Yes, we have the money for a new church but we no longer have a say in church affairs."

The new church was to be built in brick with a plaque honouring the Pioneers of Peterborough. Its architect was Miss Gwen Jones. Mrs Ruth Blair, a church stalwart, was secretary for many years and played the organ during services and at weddings. The *Camperdown Chronicle* reported:

> On Easter Sunday (1934) the Rev D.A. Cameron, who was former Moderator-General, will preach in the new Presbyterian church and Mrs MacGillivray, the oldest resident who is 90 years of age, will open the church. A concert will be held on Easter Monday night in aid of the church funds ... A dance will follow in aid of the Hall funds. There will be a good orchestra and supper.

Jessie Scott MacGillivray died at *Tulach Ard* in 1934. Only a week before her death Dr Brooke Nicholls wrote an article "Wrecks and Memories" in *The Weekly Times* about Mrs MacGillivray and her daughter, Effie. Frail she may have been but Jessie's mind was as clear as a bell. Her death was widely reported in local and Melbourne newspapers. It marked the end of an era for Peterborough.

The guest house era came to an end with the advent of World War II. Car travel had become widely available and motels became convenient places to stay. Also many of the younger generation of regular visitors wanted their own holiday houses. *Tulach Ard*, no longer in the MacKenzie family hands, burnt down, as did the *Peterborough Hotel* in 1965. *Sunny Brae* and *Blair Athol* were demolished.

Tom MacKenzie, who became as highly and fondly regarded in Peterborough as Charles MacGillivray, died in 1948. Apart from his responsibilities at *Tulach Ard* and the farm he was Postmaster for 25 years. He was a trustee of the Mechanics Hall which he and Effie had been active in building, and also its Secretary. He was an elder in the Presbyterian church, Treasurer for 40 years and attended to its maintenance. He was a member of the Foreshore and the Golf Club Committees.

After his death, Effie MacKenzie did not wish her family's pioneering stories to be lost. With her sight deteriorating, she would sit by the open fire with two lifetimes of diaries and papers, letters, photographs, newspaper clippings and articles spread about her. She and her daughter Bon sorted through the material and Bon wrote down her mother's memoirs. In 1954, after five years work, the National Press published the result of their efforts, *Shipwrecks* by Margaret E. MacKenzie. It was reviewed favourably in Melbourne and local newspapers and reprinted almost immediately and many times afterwards.

With the royalties from the first edition and assistance from her nephew, Robert Burns McKenzie, Effie restored the graves of the seamen, including the captain, who died when the *Newfield* was wrecked. The graves in Port Campbell Cemetery had become overgrown with scrub and lost to sight. Effie died in 1961. Her children and grandchildren, like those of other pioneers, continued to be active in the Peterborough community.

8

Peterborough Post Office

The MacGillivray-MacKenzie family's connection with Peterborough's postal services dated back at least as far as 1880. On Wednesday, 23 June 1880, Jessie MacGillivray wrote in her diary: "Father went for the mail today." Andrew Sorlie Macdonald had held a senior role in the Edinburgh Post Office before coming to Australia with his wife and child for the good of his health in 1841. Never one to be idle, his initiative in riding over to Port Campbell to collect the mail for people in the Peterborough district and distributing it from *Oak Bank* was the unofficial beginning of a long family association with the Peterborough Post Office. The connection lasted until 1955 when his granddaughter Aileen Row (MacKenzie) and her husband, who had built a strong business, sold to Mrs Vagg and her son Colin.

Official records from 1880 show the Peterborough postal district used the postmark 831 Port Campbell West.

From 29 May 1882 onwards, Andrew Macdonald no longer had to ride to Port Campbell to collect the mail personally as a mail bag service was introduced. But he continued to assist with distribution, for no financial return, until the first Peterborough Post Office, based at *Oak Bank*, opened on 10 April 1890. Its assigned number was 1749 and Andrew Sorlie Macdonald was appointed the first Post Master. Officially, it was known as Port Campbell West (sub branch of Port Campbell West 831.)

As records show, the responsibility for serving as Post Master or Post Mistress was subsequently passed from one of the "Mac" clan to another for generations. After Andrew Macdonald it was:

Transferred to Charles McGillivray 26 June 1893.

Transferred to Sarah Adeline Macdonald 16 February 1898.

Transferred to Mary (Molly) Isabella MacGillivray 1907.

Transferred to Flora Macdonald 1911.

Transferred from J.Milne to Tom MacKenzie 16 September 1920, with Miss Milne as his deputy and Miss Aileen MacKenzie as assistant.

Transferred from J.J.MacKenzie to Aileen Jessie Row 22 May 1944.

Transferred from Aileen Row to Ken Row 1 December 1947.

Transferred from Ken Row to Colin Vagg 1 August 1955.

Transferred from Colin Vagg to Ben Fowler 1 November 1957.

Transferred from Ben Fowler to Herbert Eales 14 December 1959.

Peterborough's isolation was relieved in 1907 when the Post Master General's Department, as it was later known, agreed a permanent telephone service was long overdue. Charles and Duncan MacGillivray had recently built a large house for Jessie's sister, Miss Sarah Sorlie Macdonald, who intended to retire at Peterborough. This house, named *Sunny Brae*, occupied one of the highest sites in the town. With Miss Macdonald's blessing, one end of the east-facing verandah was partitioned off so Peterborough Post Office was transferred from *Oak Bank* to the village.

Records show the service was warranted:

Articles Posted

	Letters	Papers	Packages
1906	7,370	612	309
1907	9, 826	610	405
1908	11,018	525	121
1909	9,757	431	361
1910	9,530	473	435

Telegrams

	Sent	Received
1906	667	397
1907	700	405
1908	970	646
1909	671	422
1910	674	451

Revenue

	Post	Telegraph	Phone	Postal Notes	Total
1906	45	40			£88
1907	60	28	14	4	£108
1908	52	46	20	5	£123
1909	61	28	15	5	£109
1910	60	30	15	4	£115

Shortly before the First World War, Effie MacKenzie began a small shop beside the Post Office, which grew to become Peterborough's General Store. The shop was initially one small room. Her account book from December 1913/January 1914 showed marmalade was 10 pence a tin, raspberry jam a shilling and vanilla 6 pence a bottle. Three pounds of rice was a shilling and a cake of soap 6 pence. One customer was charged 5 shillings for the shearing of 20 sheep.

Bardie Mercer (née Grimwade) recalled it as a hub of local activity in the 1940s:

> The only shop in Peterborough in those days was the Post Office. Such a shame they changed the look of it; it was a little weatherboard building, very dark inside, with a wide counter and one could buy essential groceries or one of the billies hanging from the ceiling. Through a grille in the wall was the actual Post Office, and there reigned Mrs Row at the telephone switchboard. Mr Row worked the other part of the business, and he was obliging.
>
> Not everyone owned cars at that time, and if people wanted to travel to Peterborough they caught the train from Melbourne to Camperdown, then a bus to Peterborough. The trip took almost all day I think. The bus would arrive in Peterborough at twenty past four each afternoon, and we would hear it clonking over the old wooden bridge. The mail came on the same bus, and the newspapers. I remember it being a long day to wait through if one was waiting for exam results in the paper.

"I have seldom seen a more fearful section of coastline"

(Matthew Flinders)

9

Scandals and shipwrecks

"I have seldom seen a more fearful section of coastline," wrote Matthew Flinders, the first explorer to circumnavigate and map Australia's coastline in 1802 and 1803. Flinders was referring to the cragged Victorian coast, where at least 638 known shipwrecks occurred, of which only about 240 were ever discovered. Peterborough, on the Great Ocean Road, is sited between Curdies Inlet and the Bay of Martyrs on a notoriously treacherous stretch known as the Shipwreck Coast which is of particular interest to divers and historians. The 130km from Port Fairy to Cape Otway contains more than 80 shipwrecks, of which the *Children* and the *Schomberg* are among the most famous.

The vessels wrecked in closest proximity to Peterborough were: the *Schomberg,* which came ashore at Curdies Inlet in 1855 after sailing too close to the coast; the *Young Australian* that came aground in a severe storm in 1877; the *Newfield* that sailed into a cliff in the early hours of the morning because the captain did not know where he was and mistook the Otway light for the King Island light and the *Falls of Halladale* that sailed into a reef in a calm sea in 1908, reputedly in a sea mist.

Further west, towards Warrnambool, the **Children** was blown off course in a severe windstorm and struck a reef at Childers Cove in

1839. The wooden barque, owned by the pioneering Henty family of Portland, was a trading ship carrying 1,500 sheep, horses, bullocks, farm equipment and house bricks from Launceston to Adelaide. Sixteen people, including its captain, drowned. After huddling on a beach, some of the 24 survivors, looking for Port Fairy, walked the wrong way east before returning and were probably the first whites to traverse that area. Finally they were taken by horse and cart to Campbell's farm, near the Port Fairy whaling station. While most of the *Children* had long been destroyed by waves, it was declared a Historic Shipwreck in 1982.

In 1845 and 1846, the Superintendent of Port Phillip District, Charles La Trobe, organised expeditions from Allansford to Cape Otway with the objective of building a lighthouse. He covered the last part of the journey on foot, being unable to take the horses through the difficult terrain. But a lighthouse was eventually built at Cape Otway in 1848. The Cape Otway Lightstation is Australia's oldest, surviving lighthouse, perched on towering cliffs overlooking Bass Strait. For generations of immigrants, it was their first glimpse of land after months at sea. (Click http://www.lightstation.com).

Ship building was highly competitive in the mid-19th century when the challenge was to design ships to sail from England to Australia in record time. In 1855, the newly built *Schomberg*, part of the Black Ball Line's passenger fleet, was described by its captain James Forbes as "the noblest ship that ever floated upon the water". The £43,103 vessel was designed and constructed in Aberdeen to beat the fast North American clippers. It was 288ft (87.8m) long, 45 ft (13.7m) wide and 29.2ft (8.9m) in depth at the hold. Its frame was British oak, with layers of Scottish larch fitted diagonally over the frame in a style similar to a new yacht designed for Queen Victoria. An outer layer of red pine was reinforced with tar. Its three masts carried 16,000 square yards of canvas sail. Below deck, first class passengers enjoyed lavish accommodation.

Launching *Schomberg,* James Baines, owner of the Black Ball Line said: "By the grace of God, this ship under the capable command of Captain Forbes will break the record he has already made." James "Bully" Forbes, a native son of Aberdeen who began his seafaring training at age 12, was reportedly drunk at the launch (perhaps an omen of unfortunate events to come). He replied, with confidence, "With or without the help of God I'll make the trip in 60 days." Forbes was a hero in England and Australia for bringing the countries closer together. Three years earlier, in 1852, he had made the Melbourne-Liverpool run in 76 days on the *Marco Polo,* carrying a 340 ounce gold nugget for Queen Victoria from the new colony bearing her name. In 1854, commanding the *Lightning,* Forbes had set a record on the Melbourne-Liverpool run of 63 days. No sailing ship ever bettered it.

*'Young Australian', three-masted schooner grounded
in Curdies Inlet, 25 May 1877*

On her maiden voyage, *Schomberg* was hampered by calm weather and windless days, especially near the Equator. It left Liverpool on 6 October 1855 with 430 passengers and 3,000 tons of cargo, mainly iron rails for the Geelong Railway and a new bridge over the Yarra to connect Melbourne and Hawthorn.

Sailing was uneventful. On the 27th day from port, Captain Forbes sighted a Liverpool-bound clipper, *Vision*. He and a boatload of passengers rowed across for an evening of dancing. When the boats parted, *Vision* took mail from the *Schomberg*'s passengers back to England.

On Christmas Eve 1855, the vessel sighted landfall near Cape Bridgewater. Moonlight Head was sighted the next day. That night, as the wind dropped, the *Schomberg* headed in towards Moonlight Head. In a gentle breeze, the vessel struggled to turn and was carried in through the breakers. It came to a grinding halt close to a circular reef, near the Schomberg rock, which is a good fishing spot in very calm weather. The vessel was only a day's sailing from Port Phillip Bay. Unfairly or not, the disaster set off a train of recriminations, rumours and inquiries.

During the night, a lifeboat was launched to locate a safe spot to land the passengers. The boat returned and the crew advised Captain Forbes to wait until daybreak because heavy surf could have easily overturned the small lifeboats. At dawn, the ship's Chief Officer saw the smoke of a distant steamer, *SS Queen*. He sounded the signal guns and *SS Queen*, which was bound for Melbourne, approached *Schomberg* and managed to take all passengers on board. Another steamer was sent to collect baggage. Various steamers unloaded the cargo from *Schomberg* but when the weather changed for the worse cargo was strewn over the beach. Police patrolled for looters.

The tragedy did not stop there. In the years after the wreck, the *Schomberg*'s cargo was on sold twice. It was not salvaged, however, mainly due to the torrid nature of the waters in which it was lost. Never was this more evident than in September 1864 when two of the new owners, Captain Seilley and Mr Hall, were drowned while sailing out to the nine-year-old wreck with the intention of raising its cargo. The *Warrnambool Examiner's* account was reproduced in *The Argus*:

> After getting safely out of the mouth of the river, an immense 'breaker' struck the boat, capsizing her, and smashing her into fragments. Of course each man at once endeavoured to make the best he could to get on shore, which was safely accomplished by the four sailors, but Mr Hall and Captain Seilley were both observed to be dead previous to that ... The boat in which the catastrophe occurred was a life-boat of five tons and arrived here (Warrnambool) from Melbourne on Sunday week ... It may appear strange that the boat should complete the voyage safely from Sandridge to Curdies River, and then get smashed to pieces in merely going out of the river; but it must be borne in mind that the "breakers" on such a coast as where the *Schomberg* lies are considerably more dangerous and of greater force than the ocean seas.
>
> It is but due also to the settlers residing on the coast, to state that including Mrs. Meek, they all were most anxious to render assistance.

The Inquest concluded that the vessel used in the expedition was "both too old and too rotten for the undertaking, and thereby mainly contributed to the loss of life which has occurred."

After that, all salvage attempts were abandoned.

Asked for his reminiscences of Peterborough, James 3rd Irvine recalled an earthquake in about 1903 that submerged the remains of the wreck. He said:

> The tide rises and the tide falls. The sand spit which goes out to the Schomberg reef when I first came here was so

high that we used to take two horses and the wagonette and take the lunches for picnics. However there was an earthquake and the whole thing disappeared and has never been discovered again. The earthquake caused a great deal of damage – all the tombstones in Warrnambool fell down.

He did not remember the exact date but it was in the early years of the 20th century.

The sand spit reappeared within a few decades, and when Michael Moore was a boy in the 1940s it was possible to walk out to the *Schomberg* at low tide. "But for many years now it has been half a kilometre of water between the spit and the Schommie. The Front Beach and the Newfield Beach are always changing with storms and tides."

Schomberg is part of the Shipwreck Coast Historic Shipwreck Trail and was protected as a Historic Shipwreck on 11 March 1982. Artefacts salvaged, by divers through the years, including belt buckles, knives and candle sticks, are displayed at the Flagstaff Hill Maritime Museum.

In Melbourne in 1856, at an inquiry into the disaster, passengers accused Captain Forbes of neglect of duty. They complained of him strutting around *Schomberg* with a loaded revolver, of "ungentlemanly conduct" among all of the officers and of "half naked women" emerging from Captain Forbes' cabin at night. He was accused of being below deck, playing cards with two female passengers when the *Schomberg* ran aground. By the time he came up on deck and gave orders, his accusers claimed, it was too late. His eventual acquittal, on the grounds of insufficient evidence to show he had not used every precaution necessary to save his ship, sparked a public outcry. He returned to England, but his career continued to decline. He died in 1874.

Historian Don Charlwood's great-grandmother, Mary Lewis, was aboard the *Schomberg* bringing her six children from London to join their father. From eyewitness accounts and transcripts of the inquiries and trial that followed, Charlwood pieced together details of the accident in his book *Wrecks and Reputations*. Sixty years after the wreck, the eldest child, Emily Lewis, at the time 17, became Charlwood's grandmother. On her 90th birthday she recalled: "We were not allowed to take any of our belongings – so I put on two dresses." Later they retrieved only two bowls, which stayed with the family in Melbourne as keepsakes. For all the drama surrounding the *Schomberg*, no lives were lost.

In 1858, the cargo ship ***John Scott*** was wrecked near to where the ***Antares*** later foundered. The *John Scott* had been carrying flour, wheat and smelted copper from Adelaide to Melbourne. After striking a reef in heavy seas, it was forced ashore at Bold Projection near Flaxman's Hill west of Peterborough. All on board were saved, the cargo was salvaged but the vessel was unsalvageable.

By the time of the next major shipwreck in its immediate vicinity, three houses had been built in Peterborough. The ***Young Australian*** was carrying sugar and rum from Queensland to Adelaide when severe storms damaged its rigging and forced it ashore in late autumn 1877.

Years later, in *Shipwrecks*, Margaret (Effie) MacKenzie) referred to the vessel as *Young Australia*, its original name that was later changed to the *Young Australian* and re-registered in Fiji to avoid Australian regulations for the importation of New Hebridean islanders, kanackers. By the time it was wrecked it was called the *Young Australian*.

Effie MacKenzie wrote:

> On the 28th May, 1877, the *Young Australia* was wrecked on the surf beach just over the sand hills from our home.

By that time my family had been some four years in Peterborough, and I was a toddler of three-and-a-half.

The *Young Australia* was a small vessel of 130 tons under the command of Captain Whitfield … In a heavy gale Captain Whitfield steered for Curdies Inlet, so successfully that his ship passed safely between the sunken reefs, and entered the tiny rock bound bay at the mouth of the river. Here she tried to anchor, but in the gale the anchors would not hold and she was washed broadside on to the beach where she was battered by the breakers until she became a total loss. One of the crew who initially tried to swim ashore with a rope was drowned.

My father (Charles MacGillivray from *Oak Bank*), the local fisherman, John Langabeer and two other men – all the small settlement could muster – hurried down to the beach to give what assistance they could. The fisherman's river boat was too small to attempt a rescue by water, and the men on shore seemed helpless, but not so the sailors. They tossed overboard a box containing a rope one of which was tied to the ship. This drifted ashore. The men quickly rescued it from the waves, and gripping the rope as in a tug-of-war made it taut. Immediately one of the sailors attempted to come in on it. However, the strength of the men was not great enough to keep him clear of the surf, and he was drowned. Then my father hurried home and brought down his horse and dray, and the weight of this, allied to the strength of the horse pulling in the opposite direction, kept the rope sufficiently taut to allow the sailors to come in safely hand over hand. The few local residents gave hospitality to the shipwrecked men. My mother's diary states – 'Mr Hill, the mate, stayed with us'.

Later the crew was taken to Warrnambool, including a young Welsh boy named Evan Evans who knew that he had a relative in the town.

After the heavy seas abated, part of the cargo was recovered – mainly casks of rum. The remains of the ship lay on the surf beach, exposed at low tide, for 50 years but it gradually became embedded in the sand until it was completely covered.

Casting new light on an old mystery

Officially, the reasons for the disaster were unclear, with the captain blaming the owner and the owner blaming the captain and crew. It is also highly likely that the owner strongly suspected the captain had sold some of the rum in Sydney, but was unable to prove it. A reappraisal of the evidence suggests the owner was almost certainly correct in his suspicions of corruption.

What is not in dispute is that the *Young Australian*, under Captain William Whitfield, made an unscheduled stop in Sydney. Captain Whitfield's claims that the vessel was unseaworthy and in need of urgent repair were picked up by the press, with one newspaper criticising the owners for operating a "seagoing coffin". But in a letter to *The Age* published on 16 July 1877 the ship's owner Andrew Muir tried to set the record straight. After buying the vessel in 1875, he had stripped it back and spent £700 on a refit. Contrary to claims it was in poor condition, its operational equipment was new and "in as good order as any vessel on the coast." While he had responded to Whitfield's request for £30 for urgent repairs in Sydney, he later found there had been no reason to interrupt the journey there with an unscheduled stop. "I can but state my firm conviction that if the rum casks could speak they could give a very lucid explanation of how the *Young Australian* was lost, and the blame could then be saddled on the right shoulders."

From newspaper reports of the time, the number of barrels of rum salvaged from the vessel would suggest a significant amount of the cargo was missing by the time the ship was wrecked. If the owner's suspicions were correct, Whitfield would have had a very good reason for sailing the *Young Australian* into the front beach at Peterborough to avoid detection for the theft. Or, at the very least, he would not have been overly upset when the mishap occurred in what was reportedly a bad storm. The issue was never resolved, for lack of proof.

The *Young Australian* had long been mired in controversy. The wooden schooner had been what was known as a "blackbirder" in the South Seas. In 1868, it had been chartered by the South Seas Trading Company to bring cheap labour from the Pacific Islands to work on Queensland's sugar plantations and Fiji's cotton plantations. As Heritage Victoria explains, the trade was so lucrative that violence and brutality were used to recruit reluctant natives:

> In 1868, while the *Young Australian* was on a recruiting voyage to supply the cotton plantations of Fiji, three natives of the New Hebrides, who had been kidnapped, were shot and murdered on board, after causing a disturbance. Following this quelling of the disturbance 230 men and six women were sold in Levuka for £1200.

After news of the shootings leaked out, the then-captain Albert Hovell (son of the explorer William Hovell) and one of his men were tried in Sydney and found guilty of murder. According to the Victorian Heritage database:

> Shipping circles were shocked and horrified that a ship's captain could have been convicted for an offence against natives. The death sentence was imposed on the two men, but later remitted to life imprisonment. Another man was found guilty of manslaughter and sentenced to seven years' hard labour. None served more than a small part of their sentences. Yet it had been due to the interference of the missionaries that the murders committed on the *Young Australian* had become known, forcing a trial.

In June 1878, 13 months after the wreck of the *Young Australian*, almost all passengers and crew aboard the **Loch Ard,** a 1700 ton three-masted iron cargo ship were lost when mist caused their vessel to run into Mutton Bird Island near Port Campbell, east of Peterborough. Only two of the 54 people on board survived. They were Eva Carmichael, an 18 year-old girl whose entire family was lost in the disaster, and apprentice sailor Tom Pearce, about the same age, who saved her life.

On Tuesday, 30 August 1892, the *Warrnambool Standard* reported another "Calamitous Wreck Near Curdies River", detailing the demise of the **Newfield.** Poor weather and faulty navigation caused the barque to be blown 70 miles off course and on to rocks on a voyage from Scotland to Brisbane carrying a cargo of salt. Captain George Scott and eight crew were drowned and 19 sailors survived, a few making seemingly miraculous escapes in lifeboats.

According to the *Standard*, the vessel struck rocks within sight of the wrecks of the *Schomberg*, the *Loch Ard*, and the *Fiji* at about 3.30am. Surviving crew members said Captain Scott "mistook the Cape Otway light for that of King Island'." The loss of life was attributed to "the unnecessary haste to leave the vessel". The *Standard* added:

> Had they only waited until daylight the probabilities are that everyone would have been saved, but believing the ship was sinking, the captain gave orders to lower the boats, and then followed a scene of confusion, every man evidently striving to get into the boats, and it was not until two life boats had been destroyed and several lives lost that the remainder of the crew thought of waiting for daylight to ascertain their position.

Daybreak brought survivors the cheering sight of houses in the distance "and a stretch of sandy beach about half a mile away."

A crowd of people had assembled on the beach and as a lifeboat approached the shore several local men pulled it to the beach.

> The *Newfield* struck a reef which extends about 300 yards from the shore and she now appears to be immovably fixed on this rock. The scene is on one of the most forbidding looking parts of the coast. Certainly the cliffs are not above 100 feet in height ... There are several small bays on either side of this rock, but the wreck is exposed to the full force of the seas, and when rougher weather sets in she will go to pieces.

> It is very gratifying to know that the survivors are well provided for. Immediately they landed, the kind people of Peterborough offered them homes for the time being. They are now located at Irvine's, Blair's, and MacGillivray's and the men appear to be faring well under the kind treatment.

The ***Falls of Halladale*** was lost near Peterborough in 1908, on the last leg of a voyage from New York to Melbourne when its captain became unsure of his location due to sea mist. With all its sails set, it struck a reef. According to Victorian government records summarised by Paradise Divers in Victoria:

> As the fog lifted, the crew and captain of *Falls of Halladale* found themselves with full sails set and billowing and only a few hundred metres from the shore heading straight for the rocks. The call "land close to the lee bow" was screamed but it was too late. Within two minutes the ship had struck a submerged reef. An eye witness said, "the ship seemed to leap from the water. In falling it seemed to jam hard and fast on the rocks". As the waves broke over the deck, the ship began to fill with water. The order "save your lives" was given and two lifeboats were hoisted clear of the ship. The lifeboats could not land directly on shore

at the wreck site but instead were rowed four and a half miles to a sandy beach in the Bay of Islands ... All made it safely to shore.

Falls of Halladale sat wedged firmly between two reefs for weeks and drew a large crowd of onlookers. One newspaper reported, "she is resting on an almost even keel with all her masts and rigging standing and with her canvas swelling out in a light breeze. She presents a most impressive sight".

After two months the ship was wrecked. Rough seas had pounded the vessel and the salvage company had blasted the ship. Much of the valuable cargo was washed ashore including a large quantity of oil, causing one of Victoria's earliest oil spills. Captain Thompson was found guilty by the Court of Marine Inquiry of gross misconduct and had his certificate suspended for six months.

Falls of Halladale, one of the last of the "windjammers" belonging to the Glasgow Falls Line, was carrying 56,000 American

Falls of Halladale, 1908

slate tiles, 500 sewing machines, iron and oil and glassware. About 20,000 of the tiles were recovered in official salvage operations between 1974 and 1986. Some are on display at Flagstaff Hill Maritime Museum where they have been used as roofing tiles on restored buildings.

Marjorie Leviny (née Good) was at Peterborough shortly after the wreck of the *Falls of Halladale*:

> Early in 1909 I vividly remember standing on the cliff round from the Blue Channel and seeing the ship lying in the water close in to the shore. The masts were out of the water. On the cliff was a tin shed in which a diver lived. He gave me biscuits from a Swallow & Ariel tin and put my feet in his huge diving boots.
>
> The beach at Crazy Kate was littered with tins of kerosene and huge rolls of white paper, I should think for newspaper. Also arched pieces of wood about three feet across and about six feet long. My father, John Good, collected a couple and put them in the bushes by the road and we collected them on the way home and put them in the garden and grew roses over them.

Through a telescope, Jessie MacGillivray also watched the salvage efforts and final destruction of the *Falls of Halladale* across the estuary from *Oak Bank*. In her diary, published a century later for the Heytesbury Historical Society by R. & J. Stevens, she wrote:

> Sunday 21 February 1909: Fine and low tide. Mr Beckett went down in his diving suit for the first time at the wreck (referring here to the *Falls of Halladale*). Did not go on board but dived between the rocks and vessel and walked along the bottom of the sea. . Saw nothing but a tank.

> Wednesday 24 February 1909: Nice cool weather but sea pretty high. There is nothing of interest from the wreck – the iron tank Mr Beckett saw underwater, he does not think belongs to the wreck of the Halladale as it is of stronger build. He saw a block 7 feet high and about 2 feet square. Maybe a rock or portion of the mast.

George MacReadie Beckett, known as Diver Beckett, who was born at Galloway Scotland in 1856 arrived at Geelong in 1885. He lived at Queenscliff and was considered the foremost deep sea diver and salvage operator in Australia at the time.

Jessie MacGillivray's diary entries also raised another interesting issue. The iron tank discovered by George Beckett, which he believed did not come from the *Falls of Halladale*, was evidence of another wreck near the vessel, in an area close to Massacre Bay, near Peterborough.

Nobody knows for sure how, when or why Massacre Bay was so named. The name was not on Superintendent Charles La Trobe's mud map of 1846, but the name of Bay of Martyrs was used prior to his trip along the coast. It is not known who, if anyone, that name referred to, either, but it was unlikely to have been so-called because of a massacre. The Bay of Martyrs covers the Bay of Islands and includes numerous rocky islands. La Trobe's mud map showed the Bay of Martyrs extending from the Bay of Islands to Cudgee Cudgee Creek (Curdies River). A sign on the Ocean Road now refers to a beach west of the *Falls of Halladale* wreck site as the Bay of Martyrs, whereas Peterborough residents have always known that beach as "Fisherman's".

Several theories abound. One theory, sometimes given to tourists, is that Massacre Bay is where whites slaughtered Aborigines. But in response to inquiries, in a letter dated 25 January 2006, the Community Development Officer for the Framlingham Aboriginal Trust, Neil Martin wrote:

... there is no documented evidence of massacres occur-
ring here (Peterborough). It may be a good idea to make
this clear. Generally massacres involved whoever could
be caught at the time. There are records of such abhor-
rent behaviour in South Australia with an Aborigine being drowned in tidal caves and women and children who
had taken refuge in swamps being found slaughtered. The
closest recorded massacres to Peterborough are within the
Otway Ranges and near Terang.

It is merely speculation, but it is very likely there was another
wreck near the *Falls of Halladale,* estimated to be from about 70
years earlier. Fewer than half the wrecks along the Victorian coast,
after all, have ever been discovered. The vessel *Skipjack* referred
to in La Trobe's 1845/46 diary may be the remnants discovered by
Beckett in 1909. The *Skipjack* was wrecked in 1843, so the timing
would fit.

La Trobe named the plain between Cudgee Cudgee (the Aborigines' name for the Curdies River) Creek and Allen's farm on the
Hopkins River near Warrnambool "Skipjack Plain" because as he
wrote in his diary, two years earlier, in 1843:

... the passage boat from Portland to Port Fairy came
ashore somewhere on this inaccessible coast which none
of them knew, but they imagined that they must, from
its appearance be off Cape Bridgewater to the west of
Portland. Five men on board, all of whom had got drunk
and overshot their port, and when they roused themselves
were off this coast. How they got ashore, no one could tell,
but by following the cattle tracks, they found their way to
Allen's.

The diary is now in the La Trobe Library in Swanston Street
Melbourne.

It is reasonable to assume that ruffians among the sealers and whalers along the western Victorian coast in the 1830s and 1840s would have caused intense friction among the local Aborigines by seeking out their women. It is also possible that an earlier ship was wrecked; its crew had landed near Massacre Bay and could have been killed by Aborigines out of revenge and the need for self-defence. One theory mentioned decades ago was that passengers and crew went ashore at or near Massacre Bay and were speared by Aborigines while drinking from a pool. There were no known white settlers in the Peterborough area prior to 1868, except for James Meek and the Buckley's Creek runs cattle farmers. The truth, however, is likely to remain a mystery.

More than five years after the wreck of the *Falls of Halladale*, the Italian barque *Antares* left Marseilles bound for Melbourne in December 1913 carrying a cargo of roofing tiles but failed to arrive. Official records show its wreckage was discovered near the Bay of Islands, west of Peterborough, after the beginning of World War I, in December 1914, by local farmers Phillip Le Couteur and Peter Mathieson. They were checking cattle near the coast when they noticed what looked like the hull of a ship below the cliffs. A police search discovered wreckage strewn around the cove and three bodies were discovered. A fortnight earlier, a young boy had seen what he had believed to be enemy fire from the Germans and raised the alarm that the area was being invaded. What he had seen was undoubtedly the distress flares from the *Antares*. The centenary of the accident was commemorated in Peterborough late in 2014.

For details of the historical Shipwreck trail click and dive sites:

http://www.flagstaffhill.com/media/uploads/ShipwreckTrail.pdf

http://www.dpcd.vic.gov.au/heritage/maritime/shipwrecks/victorian-shipwreck-dive-sites

PART TWO
Halcyon Decades

10

Building a community

Within a decade of James Irvine's opening Peterborough House, the hotel's annual fancy dress ball was a highlight of the village's social calendar. On 13 January 1899, when news reporting and acceptable terminology differed markedly from today, the *Warrnambool Standard* noted that the costumes worn at the ball the previous week "exceeded those of previous years, both in originality and picturesqueness. The most handsome costume was that of Mrs Cumming, representing 'Black and White', while Mrs Stewart as a Queensland black gin sustained the character admirably." Other "notable" costumes reported included: Puritan maid, French maid, Queen of the sea, fishwife, hospital nurse, dancing girl, flower girl, fortune teller, spoilt child, hunter, baker, clown, nigger, stockrider, mounted rifleman and cowboy.

A year before the death of Queen Victoria, residents and visitors to the south coast of the state named after her certainly knew how to enjoy themselves. On 22 May 1900, the *Warrnambool Standard* reported the 21st birthday festivities of Jas Irvine, eldest son of the hotel's owners:

> Peterborough House, Curdies Inlet, was on Tuesday evening last 15th inst, made extra gay. Mr Jas. Irvine, eldest son of the popular proprietor having attained his majority,

took the opportunity by request of his parents to submit a
list of his social circle for invitation to a ball in his honour.
The spacious dining room was artistically decorated, the
floor being splendidly prepared and the guests were the
leading dancing and musical fraternity.

Enjoyment was soon pictured on every face; visitors, with
their favourite songs, made the intervals attractive. At 12
o'clock an adjournment was made to the supper-room,
and, as some of the habitués of banqueting halls observed,
could not be surpassed.

Others had followed the Irvine's lead and established guest
houses with names reflecting the settlers' Scottish and English
roots. There was *Blair Athol* run by Helen Blair, Sarah Macdonald's
Sunny Brae, Tom McKenzie's *Tulach Ard* (meaning High Hill in
Scottish Gaelic) and Ruth Blair's *Palmyra*.

Holidaymakers, mainly from western Victoria initially and later
from Melbourne, appreciated the fishing, beaches, golf, tennis,
hunting and scenic beauty of the local attractions which remain
largely unchanged: the Arch and Murray Steps, Point Hesse, London
Bridge, The Grotto, The Crown of Thorns, The Spit, Schomberg
rock, the Front Beach, Curdies River and Estuary, Men's Pool and
Giant's Trousers. Likewise the many beaches in the vicinity of
Peterborough: Shaws Beach, The Ladies Beach, Crazy Kate, The
Blue Channel, The Well, Sand Slide, Worm Bay and Pirani's Rock,
Fisherman's and Crofts Bay extending to the Bay of Islands.

As improved roads and transport allowed families to become
more mobile, Peterborough's popularity increased. On 16 January
1917 the *Warrnambool Standard* reported:

In spite of wars and rumours of wars, lovely Peterborough
attracted the usual large numbers of visitors from Melbourne
and other centres for the Christmas and New Year holidays,
and Mr Irvine's up-to-date hostelry was taxed to its utmost

capacity, some having taken the precaution to book two months ahead. The Bench, surgery, pulpit, university and squatter's mansions were represented, all finding relief or respite from conventional life in the excellent fishing and shooting that this favourite locality affords, whilst for those whose tastes do not tend in that direction, or in walking revellers, tennis and golf tournaments were arranged. In the evenings there were several impromptu dances, but the climax was reached on Thursday 4th January, when a Cinderella fancy dress ball was given. Tickets were sold at one shilling and six pence each, the proceeds going towards the Belgian Babies Fund.

The journey, however, was not for the faint-hearted. In 1901, Mafe Tabart(nee Coy), who was born during the Boer War and named in honour of the Siege of Mafeking, one of the most famous battles of that war won by the British, gave an insight into her early childhood journeys from Terang to Peterborough:

That first trip, the teamster was Colin Irvine, who had been with father as a yardman for many years, and old Davie, and brother Fred must have been with them too. That still left a crowd of us in the double seater buggy. With a team of four black ponies. After a long stifling day through heavy forest all the way from Dixie, on a bad heavy track, with a few extra miles thrown in when we got on a wrong track. A change blew up and heavy rain fell. In the pitch dark they eventually heard the roar of the ocean. They had no idea where they were. Mother was terrified they would drive over the cliffs. They came to a fence, unharnessed and tied up the horses. Bags of chaff were pulled from under the tarps and were put under the buggy and wagon. Spare tarps were tied around the wheels for shelter from within. Mother and grandma and children crawled on to the bags of chaff under the wagon, and father and the men under the buggy.

After father had us all settled he handed round to everyone, me the baby included, a toddy of brandy. From mother's account, she spent most of the night foxing amongst us all to check our breathing. She was sure father had given us all too much brandy! As daylight broke, they found themselves a couple of hundred yards from the cliff by the Ladies Beach where we camped from then on until 1914 when the big drought stopped that wonderful venture for us.

Sir Stanley Argyle, Victoria's Premier from 1932 to 1935, holidayed at Irvine's boarding house when he was a student at Trinity College, Melbourne University, in 1896. He later wrote how he and fellow student Garnet Soilleux were attracted by the "ungetatable sort of place" where "fish were so ravenous and so numerous that one could catch a boat load in no time".

One university vacation they set off by train to Camperdown, where they hired a buggy, a driver and a pair of horses familiar with the bush track through the forest:

At last we reached the Inlet or estuary of Curdies River which gleamed weirdly in the starlight of a moonless clear sky. To our astonishment our Jehu drove straight into the water and appeared to be putting out to sea in a four-wheeled vehicle as the opposite shore was merely a black shadow some distance away in the half darkness.

They crossed safely finding a warm welcome at Jim Irvine's.

So did the Moore family 30 years later, when Jane Moore (known as Jenny in the family), widow of Michael Moore's grandfather Charles Moore, came to Peterborough in around 1916-17 with her seven children. Years later, her eldest son Charlie and his wife Connie brought horses with them on the train to Timboon, that were ridden on to Peterborough and Shetland ponies for their children Owen and Fred, born in 1921 and 1924 respectively. The

Timboon railway station

family also brought their dogs, which excelled in chasing the area's vast rabbit population into their warrens. Like many families, the Moores have continued to return ever since, grateful for the efforts of the pioneers.

In *Peterborough (As I Remember It) 1924-1939*, Owen Moore recounted:

> Many excursions were made on our ponies together and in the Bambie cart to the Strawberry Gardens and along the cliff from Crazy Kate to the Bay of Islands (there was no Ocean Road then, only a track of sorts). John and Bill Irvine during the summer season had a sleep-out situated in the area behind the Café; this Wocca Moore (no relation) shared with them and it became a meeting place for us. Wocca was an only child and much cherished by his mother and her sister. We were not allowed fire arms, but Wocca had a high powered air-rifle and the Irvine's a 410. Armed with these weapons we attempted to shoot little dotterels (with little or no success) on the estuary sands and particularly with the 410, rid the area of the ever increasing rabbit population.

As children in the late 20's and early 30's our 10 week stay at Peterborough was a great adventure. We fished, swam, played tennis and golf and went on crayfishing parties and over the years made many acquaintances. You could be certain each year there would be many returning as you did.

In the early days our evenings were taken up with playing rounders outside the Cottage where the tennis courts are today, many of the residents joining in. My brother and I attended a preparatory school, Adwalton, situated in Wattletree Road, East Malvern, in the latter part of the 20's. To our horror, we found the Headmistress/Proprietor, Miss Adderley also came to Peterborough at Christmas, so we could never escape her. She resided at the Hotel and formed the golfing brigade that included Mrs Warren Moore (Wocca's mother), Miss Warren her sister, Mrs Wasley, my grandmother and mother and others. These stalwarts ran a tournament for the young and I remember my mother saying that they dreaded being markers for some of the

Kit Tinsley (driver's seat), Moyle Breton (right rear) c. 1920

young, in particular my brother Fred who hit and ran, hit and ran, and by the time they caught up with him, they had lost count of the number of strokes he had taken.

There were a few boats that fished the estuary and sea in those early days, the ones I remember were, the Hotel boat rowed by Jim Irvine, Ronald Cumming's 14 footer with outboard and my father's 12 footer with outboard. When the River was open, which seems to have been more often than now, it was easy to go to sea, but when closed, boats had to be dragged to the front beach by horse or manpower. The estuary fishing was either trawling for trout or fishing for bream or mullet and at sea, trout, sweep and snapper. Mrs W.B. Cumming was an ardent exponent of fishing for mullet, she rowed her boat to the bend in the channel and could be seen there in all sorts of weather. I can remember some very happy occasions both on the river and ocean. At sea, weather permitting, we made trips to the Schomberg, landing on the beach and crossing to the rock, where some fished with long rods from the reef into the horseshoe and others baitsticked for crays in the numerous pools.

Crayfishing parties were legion in the late 20's and early 30's, a low tide was preferred, but even at that, some of the best reefs were under water. The tools of trade were a tee tree stick, six to seven feet long with either a rabbit, fish or meat, tied to the end very securely, a broom handle with a metal rod extension to which a copper wire snare was attached or a landing net and a dipper with a glass bottom to smooth out the water for better viewing. It would have been better if one had three arms to handle all this, but mostly we worked in pairs and I was usually with my mother who was very adept at it, and on many occasions worked in waist deep water. It was usually a full days outing and a sack full of crays would be the result. On returning to the Hotel, the catch was taken to the Café, part of the Hotel complex, also including the bar, where they were cooked and a cray supper was had by the adults later that evening. It was six o'clock closing, of course in those days, but the Hotel had another bar at the back to cover such an occasion.

In January 1926, Mary Jane Carty (1849-1932) Michael Moore's great-grandmother, visited Peterborough from Dublin and wrote her slightly wry impressions to family and friends in a series of long letters. In Peterborough, her Australian relatives were about as impressed with her comments as she was with the local strawberries:

> It was very cold and a high wind blowing, so Connie lit the fire (after dinner) and Charlie set the wireless. He has a wonderful set Willie has made, a box on a table and a wire goes out on a roof. We listened to a concert at Adelaide, and another at Melbourne and one at Queensland, 1,500 miles away, just sitting round the fire, no headphones, and you would think the men who spoke were in the room and the music …

> This morning I took a walk over the golf links to where they bathe and saw Jenny and Charlie swimming in a natural large pool. It is a small bay here, and immense boulders of rocks, evidently some volcanic eruption – in fact many miles after we left Melbourne it was all volcanic soil and stones, until you come to sand and then volcanic again and then red earth. From where I am writing there is a river to be seen running into the bay, and on the further side nothing but bush as far as the eye can see …

> Pleasure and money are my thinking the Australian Gods …

> Yesterday was a very hot day, a north wind blowing, so we remained indoors all morning and sewed. In the afternoon we went for a walk, and at night, 8 o'clock, Watty and I went to a service in the Hall held by an Irish Minister. He

lives 60 miles away, and rides on horseback through his parish which contains 40 places he preaches at.

Friday I sat on the beach in the morning and the others bathed. After lunch and a rest I did my fancy work and in the evening played bridge ...

At three o'clock Jenny took me for a drive in a four horse buggy; they were in traces. The buggy is on high wheels and has three seats across it. We drove over a rough road and through a mile or more of bush until we came to a small valley where there is a strawberry garden. They are planted on the sides of a small hill and a bungalow on the other side with a garden with roses, magnolias, honeysuckle, trumpet flower, canna, sweet pea, carnations, dahlias, large white daisies and other flowers. It was a perfect blaze of colour.

We all had strawberries and cream, but they have not the flavour or bouquet of our fruit. Then we drove further on to show me the cliffs and London Bridge, a natural formation of rock jutting out into the sea with waves dashing the arches and throwing up spray. They think me

Desmond Moore, Phyllis Moore, Sam Wood, Wocca Moore

very unimpressionable because I do not rave over their coastal scenery, but I tell them I have seen finer in Ireland and they are not pleased, as they think everything here is wonderful. We returned here safely after being driving for nearly three hours; we went about 10 or more miles.

In 1942, Peterborough local residents manned a coast watch observation post 24 hours a day. It was located in a log hut in the sand dunes west of the Ladies Beach. A telephone line was connected from the post office. A coast watch was conducted by local volunteers, men and women, who watched for enemy aircraft and shipping. The walls of the hut were adorned with pictures and drawings of all aircraft and shipping to identify the enemy from ours. Those who served on coast watch duty, whose efforts deserve to be acknowledged, perhaps with some kind of memorial were: Elizabeth Irvine, Bill Evans, J.G. Irvine, Aila J. Row, Tom McKenzie, Bonnie MacKenzie, Isabella Irvine, Betty MacKenzie, Betty Whitehead, Annette Breton, Effie MacKenzie, Ada Cumming, B.R Wooster, K. McKenzie, Jack Holland, R.J. King, A.E. King and Mary Weibye. They served 24 hours a day in 2-6 hour shifts and kept a record of meteorological and general observations.

Their timesheets, still preserved, attest to their conscientiousness, showing shift changes at 6am, 10am, 2pm, 6pm and midnight on some days, with changes at 9pm and 2am on others. Most people devoted several hours a day to their duty. Their observations were recorded in this style: "Friday January 23rd 1942. 10.10am approx. OBSERVED. One aeroplane, about five miles east of observation post, travelling due south, fairly high, seen and heard."

At 6am one morning in February the watcher on duty noted: "*Very* cold, rather thick mist over river. North wind."

11

And the bath was full of crayfish

MICHAEL Moore's memories of Peterborough go back to the early 1940s, as early as he can remember anything at all:

It was the place our family went for holidays in January each year for two weeks or so. The war was on; petrol rationing meant we had to save fuel coupons to have enough fuel to get the car started. We had a Chevrolet car with a gas producer mounted on the rear. These were commonly used appliances with a big iron box which was filled with charcoal. The box was mounted on a hinge and could be swung to the side to allow access to the boot.

The fire in the box had to be lit about 30 minutes before leaving and enough heat generated to produce the gas to switch over from petrol as soon as possible. Extras bags of charcoal were carried on the top of the car. The car would get up to a speed of about 25mph on the charcoal gas. If the speed dropped we had to stop and either fill up the box with extra charcoal or stoke up the fire by inserting an iron poker down the middle and move it from side to side to make the fire burn quicker. Later in the war years my father had a wheat box placed on the top. When the car reached 25 mph, a button beside the driver's door was pressed and wheat would flow into the fire box. This would increase the speed of the car to 30 mph.

The trip from our farm at Diggers Rest north of Melbourne to Peterborough took all day with a lunch stop and stops for punctures which were more frequent then because of the poor quality rubber on the tyres and tubes. Those January days were hot, and on one occasion many cars had caught fire along the Princes Highway from Melbourne to Colac, starting grass fires. The bags of charcoal on top of the fire box could catch fire and burn the whole car.

The fun route for us was through the Stoney Rises west of Colac. The road through this volcanic area had huge dips in it and the car picked up speed on the down and gave a 'big dipper' feeling as it went through the bottom.

The 'Cottage' on the corner of Mac's and Irvine Street with

Michael Tinsley, Jane Tinsley, Deborah Grimwade, Michael Moore, Peter Horsman, c. 1942

its prickly boxthorn hedge in front, always had reserved rooms for us and was an annex to the *Peterborough Hotel* on the opposite corner.

... Breakfast, lunch and dinner were provided for all guests in the dining room of the hotel, on the north east corner of Irvine and Mac's Streets. Meals were quite a social occasion, but you had to be in on time otherwise miss out. In those days crayfish were very plentiful and sometimes guests were able to catch enough for everybody. If you caught your own, Tom, the hotel handyman, would boil them over a fire outside the back of the kitchen in an old iron tank and you could have them served in the dining room. As it was easy to catch trout these were also popular and Ruby Wiber, the Hotel owner's wife would arrange for them to be cooked for breakfast. John and Ruby Wiber had taken over running the hotel from James 3rd and Isabella Irvine in 1938.

Trout could be caught trolling in the river channel up from the bridge or at the river mouth up along the surf from the front

As children we took everything at Peterborough for granted – we knew that next year it would be the same, and it always was.

beach. The way to catch trout was with a 'Warrnambool spinner'. This special hook was about three inches long with brass along the side. You had to polish the brass by rubbing it in the sand before going fishing so the shine would attract the fish. A swivel helped the spinner to turn. In those days mostly the river was open during January so you could use the outboard motor to boat out to sea. Boats were kept mostly in the river just north of the bridge.

Looking back on her holidays, another regular childhood visitor, **Soos Graansma (nee Joyce)** recalled:

As children we took everything at Peterborough for granted – we knew that next year it would be the same, and it always was. That was its charm, and why everybody came back year after year. The beautiful unspoiled, deserted beaches and so many of them to choose from superb swimming and surfing, or just racing about in the sandhills, a perfect holiday place if you preferred a simple, informal way of life. This is beginning to sound like a travelogue, but having spent ten years in Europe and having literally nowhere to spend a summer holiday but at polluted, overcrowded resorts, with little charm, I now realise just how important such a holiday place as Peterborough is.

Bardie Mercer (Nee Grimwade) remembers the hotel dining room in the 1930s and 1940s as a place where "the menu never changed and we were quite happy with roast beef or roast mutton every night. And the glee when dessert was Mrs Wiber's esmerelda rolls covered in golden syrup and cream. The dining room at the pub was a lovely room really, with a pressed tin ceiling and windows looking out over the beach. The tables all had starched white cloths and we used starched white napkins. Each table seemed to be taken up by a family, and when there was a little child a high chair would be put in place." Two sittings were held each evening, and guests dressed for dinner.

The Café, as it was known, was part of the hotel but in a separate building. It housed the bar, where adults would have a drink before dinner and children a glass of lemonade. At the back of the Café was what was known as the Cupboard, where some would disappear for a quiet drink on Sundays. On occasions when a constable from Port Campbell turned up the Cupboard would be shut in an instant and the drinkers were found just sitting around and smoking in the Café. In the 1950s, the nearby Café was the headquarters of the "PPBC" (Peterborough Power Boat Club) and the centre of some

lively drinking and hearty singing as
leading members of the club strode to
the 'stage' and sang the best parts from
HMS Pinafore.

And the bath was full of crayfish.

Rosemary (Posy) Durham (neé Grimwade) recalled the crayfish – a bath tub full of them in the 1950s at what had locally become known as the House of Sin:

> I will never forget the day I realised that our House of Sin had passed on to the next age group ... I strolled into the house to find Will Kelly and Andy Gubbins having an earnest discussion on girls – Andy announced in loud, clear tones, aged 14 "I will NEVER get married, I am a misogynist person." And the bath was full of crayfish.

By today's standards, the so-called House of Sin's inhabitants were usually models of good behaviour. The property, in Robertson Street, was owned by the Kelly family from the Western District and a number of young bachelors used to regularly stay there and have drinking parties. It probably fell down from neglect after Will Kelly was tragically drowned in 1963 while pulling a cray pot near the sand slide on Christmas Day.

Marjorie Leviny (née Good) was just nine months when she was first taken to Peterborough in the first decade of the 20th century:

> We used to go down with what Mother called a wagonette, but I don't remember much difference to a four-wheel cart. There must have been as the luggage was considerable. We went from Injemira, Grasmere, taking a baby's bath, cot, methylated spirits, iron, nurse, etc. The dust would rise up and pour into the cab and I would be sick. Sometimes we had to cope with bushfires. I also remember planting marrum grass with Mother and Jim Irvine, in front of the Hotel by the river on the sandhill.

Jane Dyson, nee Tinsley, c. 1952

Peterborough was still a day's journey from Melbourne in the 1940s, when **Jane Dyson (née Tinsley)** travelled down with her family:

> It always took a whole day to get there, leaving straight after breakfast and having a picnic lunch at Colac or in the Stony Rises. All the sign posts had been removed, so the Germans or Japanese wouldn't be able to find out where they were, or where Peterborough was. We thought Mum was marvellous knowing which red gravel road to turn along.

We wore shorts, shirts and knitted woollen jumpers ... All the children wore leather "Roman" sandals, which had an ankle strap over the instep which could be tightened or loosened with a buckle. Our bathers were made of some incredibly scratchy woollen stuff, usually dark red or blue, and it would get matted thick with salt water and sand.

The Hotel lavatories, three for gentlemen and three for ladies, were about 20 yards up separate paths behind the Hotel. They were weatherboard, whitewashed every so often and the whitewash was flaky and peeling. You could climb over the partition between each lavatory and then wriggle out under the last lavatory door, this would leave all three locked from inside, and make the grown-ups very cross.

Very cross indeed!

Few new houses were built in Peterborough during the war years, until development stirred again in the post-war boom years of the 1950s.

12

A character and a gentleman

HOWEVER spectacular its scenery and however rich its history, the essence of Peterborough has always been the colourful, interesting personalities who have shaped its story since the mid-Victorian era. Aware that this book has been in the pipeline for a long time, a number of "old timers" recorded their memories and those of other townspeople, with warmth and affection. One much-loved resident whose name cropped up frequently was **Moyle Breton**, popularly known as **Breet, the Bosun, Baldy** or **Wigley.** He was one of a kind and unforgettable for all who enjoyed his company.

Moyle was a storyteller, fisherman, professional golfer, wartime soldier, occasional eccentric, saxophone player, a deeply faithful Christian and especially important to several generations of children who grew up or holidayed in Peterborough. He was variously described as "lively, kind, never swore, always full of fun and utterly fascinating."

Moyle's father, **Dr Prosper Breton**, was the Terang doctor for many years and he and his wife **Annette** educated their sons, Moyle and Hewlett, at Geelong Grammar School. In Terang, Dr Breton played the violin, Mrs Breton the piano, Moyle the saxophone and Hewlett the banjo. Later, in Peterborough, Moyle played with Todd Sloane's band on important social occasions. Annette and the boys moved permanently to Peterborough after Dr Breton's death, living on the corner of Mac's and Blair Streets in a comfortable, modest weatherboard home.

Moyle worked for several years as a fisherman and also as a professional golfer. With a crystal clear memory of childhood holidays, **Jane Dyson** (née Tinsley) recalled Moyle's compelling, tall stories. He told her and the many children who befriended him "about Japanese tortures, about how he stood on his hands on the edge of the Geelong Grammar tower, about pirates, about ghosts, about fishing ... you name it, and he had a story." He took groups of children exploring the local area, outings they regarded as real adventures. From the perspective of a child, he was a "completely magical grown-up".

Soos Graansma (Joyce) remembered:

> As small children we hung on his every word – and did he have some stories to tell. I can remember all sitting around him in a large circle of 10 or 12 children, all spell-bound. How we loved Breton. As we grew older, he became a

Soos Gransma

little more reckless and loaded us back into the back of his Land Rover and went roaring up the front road to stop only a few inches from the cliff edge – not loved by our parents, needless to say!

Duncan McNab observed Moyle's legendary skills at sea:

> He always sat up in the bow wedging his broad back against the canvas cover, with his old captain's cap on and a pair of old sandshoes. His eyes never really left the sea for a minute and he always held the anchor rope in his hands when we were sweep fishing, just letting the boat pull against his hands and not snap on the anchor rope. He had an unusual or even rare ability to read trouble and on lots of occasions would call out suddenly "start the motor", and sure enough a minute or two later there would be a big swell go through.

> Breton at sea was at home, much more so than on the land. He loved it and understood it, he was very knowledgeable and very careful, and spanning three or four generations, easily the safest and cleverest of the Peterborough sea men, nobody ever argued with him at sea.

After ending his career in professional fishing Moyle rarely ventured out, and only for sweep. On those occasions, **Duncan McNab** recalled, "it was a pleasure to see his hands almost like a musician as the line ran through, always in control but very little sudden movement. He was a great fisherman."

Andrew Chirnside was undoubtedly right when he said Moyle could have written a best seller if he had been so inclined. Among the assorted goodies at the Bretons' home was Dr Breton's old medical kit. "It was all kept in a very large wooden chest and on special occasions Breet would open this chest and explain which knife was used to cut a leg or arm off some pirate who had been wounded in some horrendous battle." Andrew recalled:

I remember driving along in his jeep with four or five other children all singing at the top of our voices. How could children not love a man like this? Happily many other children followed on to share Breet at his best.

World War II, however, as Andrew said, "came and interrupted this utopia as my father and Breet enlisted". Moyle joined the army. "He was in Darwin when Japan entered the war and was in an ack ack division when the Japs bombed the town. Later he told us how he had shot down most of the Japanese Air Force, which went to further our hero worship."

In his *Memories of Peterborough in the 1950s*, **John Bartlam** recalled Moyle in the thick of the fun as a member of the famous PBBC (Peterborough Power Boat Club), performing *HMS Pinafore* at the *Peterborough Hotel* Café. Moyle played the "Bosun".

Moyle was also notorious, as Wocca Moore noted in 1971,

> … for his bull terrier, aptly named 'Boodling Pup'. This dog loved to approach you in a completely unemotional way, no snarl, no bark, no wag of the tail and then hold you by the calf in a grip of steel. It removed one whole leg of Judge Wasley's new grey trousers on one occasion. It had an eye for romance too! About sunset on a summer eve, the silhouette of Breet (Moyle) and his current fiancé, followed at one hundred paces by Sammy Dunlop, followed by Boo at a further one hundred paces, could often be seen walking along the cliff top in the direction of Poddy's Lookout and the marram grass. Breet for a time just after the war removed to Princetown, where he settled on a bleak and wind-swept sand hill. There he shared a square concrete room, a mahogany four poster and an oak fishing dining table with Boo and 32 ferrets.

Annette Breton was also an unforgettable personality, the maker of birthday cakes for her many friends. **Andrew Chirnside** remembered:

Mother Breton as she was known to all at Peterborough and beyond was the closest thing to a saint that most will meet. She was without doubt the finest of ladies with a quick wit, a marvellous laugh and sense of humour. Mother was deeply religious, as was Breet. I never heard him blaspheme, and he swore on very few occasions.

Mother always played the organ in the local church and Breet collected the plate. There were occasions when the entire congregation consisted of the Minister, Mother and Breet. This did not however detract from her playing, it was always as though she was playing in St Paul's.

Prue Holden in her *Stories of Peterborough and the Staughton Family* of the 1920s wrote of **Annette Breton**, who died in 1967:

I always loved staying with Breatie (Annette), she was mother's best friend and they visited each other a lot, but even so they always called each other Mrs Breton and Mrs Staughton. My memories of Breatie were that she was so full of life and such a personality and my Mother said that even when she cried she never cried the way that other people did, the tears just rolled down her cheeks and her face didn't crumple up or look ugly. When we came to call on her she always complained about her old shoes. She probably had painful feet and perhaps that is why she wore sand shoes that she dyed purple. Sad to say I only saw her a few times when I grew up.

Prue remembered being teased "like mad" by Moyle. He suffered from asthma but it improved when he would stay with her family at *Keayang*, inland from Peterborough. "I thought him very clever as he said that if he put his ear to the ground he could hear all kinds of things very far away. He could make a fantastic goanna face."

Until his health failed a few years before his death in 1987, Moyle remained one of Peterborough's best-loved characters.

13

Two special young ladies

"Oh, won't it just be a day for us when this vile war ends and all our boys come back to us again. May this year see the end of it all." So wrote **Ruth Cecilia Affleck** in early 1918. Ruth, who was born in 1901, grew up on Minjah station near Warrnambool, was educated at Clyde Girls School at Woodend, and holidayed at Peterborough. Her vibrant jottings, penned around the time she left school and a few years before she married another regular Peterborough visitor, grazier **Harold Thornton (Tinny) Grimwade**, a founding member of the Peterborough Power Boat Club, reflected her zest for life. Throughout 1918, various references in her diary suggested she corresponded with several of "our boys" at the front and followed the progress of many of the locals:

> Heard Ron Austin taken prisoner by Turks ... Heard of dear old Geordie's death of wounds in France, evening very painful ... Saw procession through the streets and gave the soldiers biscuits and apples ... All the dear soldiers left for Sydney (April 1918).

Finally, by November 1918, the news had brightened:

> Splendid war news, very cheering ... Austria has surrendered ... Monday 11th Heard peace was declared. Armistice signed on General Foch's terms.

Ruth worked hard assisting her father on the property: "Did cattle most of the day ... Dad and I mustered Dairy ... Rode Rua to Stallions and brought in the sheep, fearfully hot and muggy ... Got up at six and rode Rua to muster ... killed snake ... made butter ... Dad and I drove out and planted trees in new plantations ... Dad and I laid fox trails ... In afternoon found Mayhap with angelic foal." Occasionally they hunted and shot ducks, quail and rabbits.

Ruth also played hard, especially at Peterborough, where she "never enjoyed anything so much" as partying, horse riding, swimming and surfing, tennis, golfing, dancing until the small hours, crayfishing, playing bridge, gymkhanas and reading. At the end of 1918, the list of books she had read during the year, dominated by Kipling, the Brontes and other classic writers, was a credit to her teachers and her interest in literature.

A century on, her own writings bring the Peterborough of 1918 and 1919 alive. In the midst of an idyllic summer at Peterborough she mused:

> I will never have such a good time again ... and afterwards everything will be different. Of course in the far future I may have just as much fun again, but I will always look back on this year at Peterborough as one of the happiest times I have ever spent.

Her holidays were busy and eventful:

> Went out crayfishing to the Schomberg. I got 56 ... rode over to Glenample, had lunch on the beach and a glorious swim ... Shot rabbits ... Left about 11 and rode all along the coast to Sherbrooke and had lunch there, which Mrs McA brought out in a buggy, then rode to the Strawberry Gardens for tea and home in time to take the nags into the surf ... Danced and had supper in the cafe ... had lessons in new fox trot from Mrs Robertson and sang ... Had greatest

fun and just adored it … stayed out late at night and got an awful strafe.

Ruth had originally come to Peterborough at just six weeks with her mother. "I was rolled in a shawl and carefully laid on the beach." Her mother had first visited Peterborough in the late 19th century. "An old letter describes how she was rowed in the Bay by a stripling youth named Jim Irvine. She never got over her love of the place, and brought we three children down here every year, where we stayed at Irvine's Hotel." In 1914 Ruth's father bought a cottage, where the family holidayed for many years.

Decades later, Ruth's daughter, **Posy (Rosemary) Durham** (née Grimwade), and her children maintained the tradition into a fourth generation:

> If Peterborough is in your blood you can't escape. Seven-teen years after we have our own house where Tulach Ard

Cecilia Mann, Les ..., Marsali Campbell, Roy McCaughey,
Ruth Affleck, Bob McArthur

used to be and so the tradition goes on. Peterborough's charm continues, basically I hope it never changes …

Posy's sister **Bardie Mercer** (née Grimwade) recalled the dining room of the *Peterborough Hotel*: "We used to play ping pong and pump away at the old pianola while waiting for the gong to ring at

Roy McCaughey, Ruth Affleck

6.00 sharp each night." Bardie also recalled **the Misses Blair, Lily and Mary Jane**, who ran *Blair Athol* guest house on the southwest corner of Blair and Robertson Streets during the 1930s: "They milked their cows round the back of the guest house and we used to go billy in hand, every day to get the milk."

As a child, Bardie and her contemporaries were taken on boat trips from Peterborough and on trips to London Bridge, Arch and Murray Steps, Deany Steps or Loch Ard Gorge. "All ages, and nannies went along." Afternoon teas were enjoyed at the beach, with billy cans and firewood lugged along, as well as enamel mugs and tins of Christmas cake in picnic baskets.

The girls' father, "Tinny Grimwade" was remembered warmly by **Todd Sloane**, who ran Todd Sloane's Dance Band from Terang. "Mr Grimwade would be at some of the balls and as he danced past the band he would shout 'play *Bye Bye Blackbird*, Todd'." On one occasion, he brought along two large fish, to trade for a "blackbird". And when he booked the band for the wedding of one of his daughters he signed the letter "Bye Bye Blackbird."

A contemporary of Ruth Affleck's who experienced Peterborough from a different perspective was **Tess Jarvis.** Tess was born in 1910, left school at 13 to work at the *Peterborough Hotel*. Her shifts generally started at 6am and often involved scrubbing the dining and other rooms on her hands and knees. Mrs Irvine, whom Tess admired, taught her the finer points of setting a table.

Many years later, Tess shared her memories: "Started work (at the *Peterborough Hotel*) at 6am." She admired Mrs Irvine who taught her to set tables. She started as a waitress in the dining room with one table, as she learned she was given responsibility for up to three tables. On busy days, five girls would be employed in the dining room.

Tess recalled that as a child, her parents would travel to Warrnambool in a horse and cart for supplies, taking one child only.

They would also sell the peas her father grew for three shillings per pound. They would leave Nirranda about 2am, breakfast at the Junction Hotel, Allansford. They would then stock up flour, sugar, tea, rice, etc, and arrive home after midnight:

> When the hotel was open over the summer, Tess and four other girls served in the dining room. Their uniforms matched those of the housemaids of *Upstairs Downstairs* – black dresses with a white caps, aprons, collars and cuffs, well starched and ironed. In winter, Tess would return home and help on her parents' farm. Her father, who played the banjo mandolin, was a local "one man band" for dances and social occasions. Mrs Jarvis was the local midwife.

> Saturday was the day for treats, when a local shopkeeper in Peterborough would save the Ginger Meggs comics from the *Saturday Sun* for the Jarvis children. Tess had four sisters and five brothers and attended the local Nirranda School, travelling the four miles by pony or foot. Arriving soaking wet after a downpour one morning, the children were sent home. The next morning on the way to school they swished dam tree branches over themselves, hoping for another holiday.

14

Holiday fishing and a few romances

Ruth Affleck's diary references to catching crayfish reveal a great deal about fishing in Peterborough early in the 20th century, long before professionals arrived and almost fished the place out. With no boats with outboard motors before World War II, fishing was restricted to rods off the beaches and cliffs and crayfishing, plus fishing from the banks and rowing boats. Over the course of a month in the summer of 1919, Ruth recounted the number of crayfish she had caught: 78 on Sunday, January 12th, 56 on Tuesday, January 28th, 14 before breakfast on Sunday, February 2nd, and 68 at the Schomberg on February 17th.

Writing in 2000, **Joan Densley** looked back on fishing at Peterborough in the late 1930s and after the war. As a young girl, her love affair with the Bay of Islands began in 1938:

> Prior to this my seaside visits had been limited to the open beaches of Port Fairy and Warrnambool, so the sight of these majestic islands and high cliffs, indented with little coves, was quite magical.
>
> Alongside the loveliest of these sheltered beaches stood a small tin hut, the erstwhile home of a fisherman named **Teddy Collins** with whom a certain **Charlie Densley** from Terang often went to sea. Sadly the sea he so dearly

loved eventually claimed Teddy, and his hut and the lease of the Crown land on which it was situated were put up for auction, with Charlie being the winning bidder. Thus began the picnic day trips from Terang as Charlie and his son Harry (my future husband) proceeded to double the size of the hut … and the day trips became weekends.

Harry and I married just prior to the war starting in 1939, and as he was a member of the 23/21st Militia Unit he was called up for duty right away; so we rarely saw the place for the duration, and sadly Charlie didn't see it again as he died in 1945.

Post war, Joan, her two children and Harry Densley embarked on further extensions. As these continued, she and the children enjoyed various holidays there with their friend **Joyce MacKenzie** and her daughter Sandra and neighbour **Jack Haugh** and his family from Morwell. "Our children grew up together and formed life-long friendships as they played the glorious days away on 'our' beautiful little beach."

The sea, Joan recalled, "seemed full of beautiful fish and crayfish in those far off halcyon days and I remember one weekend in particular, when Jack Clifford (Terang) and I set out with Jack Haugh in his sturdy boat with a little outboard motor and made two five mile trips to the wreck of the *Antares* with a resulting bounty of 250 sweep (still the tastiest fish in the ocean, though I scarcely ever see one these days)."

From Joan's point of view, the tranquility she cherished was shattered when roads were upgraded, bringing spearfishermen and vandals – the former wreaking havoc on the crayfish and the latter breaking into homes and stealing. "Worse still some took to spending nights in our beds (ugh) but I discouraged this by strategically placing up-ended drawing pins under the sheets – with the electricity turned off they were hard to find!!"

Ross Paton also looked back on holidays at Peterborough with fond memories:

> It will always hold a soft spot for me as it was beside the 7th tee that I proposed to my wife – thankfully she accepted and we got married. We were great friends with **Mervyn** and **Ila Murnane** and we used to all go to Peterborough together quite often, staying in Laurie's hut.
>
> Mervyn had an organ in his shack and on Christmas Eve each year we would load it on to my truck and go down into town and Merv would play Christmas carols. We would drive around the village and stop in front of each house, Ila, Glenice, Merv and self, singing carols as though our lives depended on it. Hospitality was wonderful, John Wiber would make sure we didn't go dry. Other people, if in residence, one could depend on for a drink would be Tinny Grimwade and the Rod Calverts.

As a small boy in the 1920s, **A. Warren (Wocca) Moore** mustered the cows and calves for the Misses Blairs and for the MacKenzies. The animals used to roam at will over all unenclosed spaces. He would drive them "flat to the boards around the corner between the Pub and the Cottage at precisely 9.15 o'clock every morning – at that hour most of the Pub guests were either crossing the front putting green or returning to the Cottage".

He recalled the name **"Snip-Snip"** being bestowed on Tom Farley "because of Tom's habit, when trimming the box thorn hedge in front of the Pub, of punctuating each sentence spoken to passers-by with just two swift and professional snips at the hedge, "Good morning Mrs Cumming (*snip snip*), I believe you got another fox yesterday? (*snip snip*). Fine pack of dogs you have, (*snip snip)*. Good morning Mr ...""

Wocca, whose full name was Arthur Warren Moore, was from a grazing family from Womboota in NSW, near Echuca. Wocca was one of the legends of Peterborough. He flew an RAAF plane over Peterborough during World War II. He and his wife June, who was over 95 and still living in Peterborough in 2014, had two daughters, Diana and Deborah and a son, "little Wocca" who tragically died in a fire many years ago.

Apart from the Warren Moores, the many other Moores (no relation) who have enjoyed Peterborough for generations – my family – are descended from retailer Charles Moore, who died in

Wocca Moore, Owen Moore, Jim Irvine

1916. It was around that time that his widow Jane (called Jenny in the family) first brought their seven children to Peterborough. They were Charlie, Nora, Ken, Kathleen, Denis, Desmond (my father) and Patricia Moore.

Graham Murfett also mustered cows for the Misses Blairs during his holidays in the 1940s when the family stayed at *Blair Athol*. He and his cousin "would get up early each morning and herd the cows into the milking shed for Miss Blair, then too crippled to milk." Helen Blair, who died in 1926, had moved in to *Blair Athol*, originally Jemima Robertson's *Big House* on the corner of Blair and Robertson Streets in 1892 and had bought the property by 1894. It was later run by her daughters Lily Ann Blair who died in 1948 and Mary Jane Blair who died in 1956.

In the 1920s, Graham's father had also holidayed at Peterborough during the school year, not during the Christmas holidays. Graham related they stayed at Mrs Ruth Blair's guest house *Palmyra* on north east corner of Blair and Robertson Streets, where the local children were given school lessons. Mrs Ruth Blair, who died in 1961 ending her family's connection with Peterborough, had bought the site of the *Palmyra* boarding house in 1917.

While most holidaymakers stayed at the hotel or one of the boarding houses, some families camped, including the **Coy** family, which is why **Marj Leviny (née Good)** initially mistook them for gypsies:

> I remember the Coy's camp with wagon, tents and horses tethered beside the sandhill at the top of the cliff where the town ends, and the beach below is the southern extension of Crazy Kate. Phyl Coy told me there was always a baby in the crib under the wagon. I always thought they were sort of gypsies.

Johnny Bartlam was one Peterborough resident who watched the changes in his beloved "tiny, isolated windswept seaside village

Wocca Moore, Rod Calvert, John Irvine

on the south-west coast of Victoria that for several generations had a social impact far beyond its humble appearance."

For him, it was "a story as poignant as that of the passing of the age of Camelot".

Like any good Greek play, Bartlam wrote, Peterborough had a period of late-flowering decadence that flourished with the "Peterborough Power Boat Club" (that was as much an excuse for a good party as a serious attempt to promote a boat race.) Over the years, in his eyes, as roads improved, the population increased and new houses were built, a little of the early magic vanished:

> Today the coastline is as beautiful as ever, the golf course has been improved, tourists pour through along the Great Ocean Road and the sand dunes and cliff tops are decked out with walking tracks, with solemn and politically

correct signs ... however the feeling we "early people" cannot help is a sense of loss, accentuated year by year as more of the cast of *HMS Pinafore* pass away.

The various collections of marvellous photographs recall "spectacular fishing catches from out in the bay and crayfish the size of small dogs; of years when the river never opened and sand covered all the reefs far out beyond the Men's Pool; of years when the river was so wide and fast-flowing that you could easily understand why old James Irvine could be sucked under with his horse team and drowned".

These days, many of the faces are different in our little seaside village, with little hint of what was once a unique antipodean "summer place".

15

Good sports

SPORTS, including fishing, shooting and tennis, have long been favourite pastimes of generations of Peterborough's holiday-makers
and residents. The town has also had a share of organised sporting
clubs, with golf remaining the most popular.

Teeing off

SCENIC oceanside golf courses are an asset to any country. Think
of Pebble Beach in California, Ballybunion on Ireland's rugged
Kerry coast and the stunning courses of the Hawaiian islands.
Peterborough's nine hole clifftop course, with front/back nine tees
located on the same teebeds, is one of Australia's most spectacular.
Peterborough is the shortest course in the region, but it is a challenge,
especially on windy days.

Communal golf was played at Peterborough on the common
foreshore from 1893 onwards. The Irvine family pioneered golf
in Peterborough with James Irvine's family, as proprietors of the
Peterborough Hotel, establishing the original course so many
enjoyed in the early years of the 20th century. Their golf course
was built over nine holes in 1903 for their hotel guests and used
until 1932. The first tee began in front of the hotel and continued
with plenty of variety. It included Irvine's cow paddock, where the

camping ground is now. Barbed wire fences were built to keep the cows off the course, forcing golfers to crawl through the barbed wire to putt. From there the course proceeded across Hamilton Street, Robertson Street and Schomberg Road to the Ladies Beach then across the foreshore from the Men's Pool back to the Village Green in front of the Hotel, with the last tee at the top of the cliff, where the path to the front beach begins.

From the outset, the sport was popular with men and women. In her 1918 diary, Ruth Grimwade (née Affleck), the mother of Peterborough residents Posy Durham, Bardie Mercer and Deborah McNab recalled:

> There were lots of golf tournaments, but none of us won any of them. I played one with Dad, one with Max, Mr Clarke, Ford and others. I got second in the Ladies singles, I did the second best score, both gross and net. My golf has improved as Dad has been awfully good and got me two new brasseys, a mid-iron and a mashie.

In 1919 she wrote: "Boy, Reg, Edith and I played golf. Geoff came down again. Played with Desmond Moore in golf tournament and did 61-51, very brilliant." A golf professional was available for lessons in the summers of the 1920s and 1930s. Fred Moore recalled receiving lessons in the 1930s from Colin Campbell, who later became a well-known television golf commentator. By then, Blair's Boarding House had established its own golf course of six holes from Blair Athol west, extending south around the foreshore of Crazy Kate to Post Office Beach. From 1932 onwards, this was joined with the Hotel course to create a 12 hole course.

Interest and maintenance lapsed during World War II and it was not until the late 1950s, largely through the efforts of John Irvine from *The Lodge* farm, that the course was resurrected. D.H. Bradshaw recorded in his account of the *History of Peterborough*

Golf Club that the club was refounded by local residents and regular holidaymakers in 1958, with much of the initial work carried out by volunteer labour. Grazier Rod Calvert, a regular holidaymaker, was president of the revived club and his cottage was the base for meetings. John Irvine was the captain, retired shire engineer H. Cochrane was secretary. Initial subscriptions were two guineas.

Bill Rogers, a former director of BHP and a Melbourne lawyer recalled that John Irvine set about revitalising the sport by initially establishing five holes along the cliff:

> The 1st hole (is) now used only for the Fred Moore trophy, 2nd the existing 2nd and 3rd, the existing 3rd but with the tee down below and to the side of the present tee, the 4th was the present 4th and the 5th back to the third green. There was no elevated tee for the 5th.

> In those makeshift times the Calvert's house was, "by invitation," the Club House. The Calvert garage was the parking spot for golf clubs. The present car park was a swamp. "Boy" Armstrong owned the house which has become the present Club House and my recollection is that he died in the late 1950s and his widow offered the house to the Golf Club for £8,000. The Club had little or no money and Rod Calvert, John Irvine and myself guaranteed an advance from the bank for the purpose.

> Gradually the course was extended to nine holes but the elevated tees on 1st, 3rd, 5th and 9th holes were added and then added again. In the early 1960s I was appointed Senior Vice President I think by the captain, I was a member of the committee almost from the outset but seldom received notices of meetings ...

> As the Golf Club developed, the key social event of the summer was the Fred Moore trophy played over 12 holes, mixed foursomes and no handicaps.

That event was played during the "ANA" weekend as was a tennis mixed doubles event and a cricket match against a local team at Port Campbell. Swimming races were part of the fun in the 1920s and 1930s at the Blue Pool, also known as The Channel. In the 1950s, there was also a fancy dress dance in the hall, until it blew over.

The nine hole golf course is situated on the southern and western part of the Foreshore Reserve and extends south of Schomberg Road and north along the eastern side of Crazy Kate. The last hole is near the Club House in Schomberg Road. One of the major golf competitions now conducted by the Golf Club is the Schomberg Cup. This was originally the annual boat race run around the bay off the front beach conducted by the Peterborough Power Boat Club in the 1950s.

Casting off

In the late '40s, the Peterborough Power Boat Club (PPBC) was formed. The original crew were: Des Moore as admiral; Warren (Wocca) Moore as captain; hotel proprietor John Wiber as bosun; and Andy Chirnside as chief engineer. Many other officers and crew were added later, including Tinny Grimwade as lieutenant commander and Bill Holbeach as able seaman "wader" because his boat was swamped in the surf. Tom Austin was the ship's cat, but later graduated to ordinary seaman, John Moore was the chief writer. For some arcane reason peculiar to the era, female members were addressed as "Seagull". The main objective of the PPBC was the running of the Schomberg Cup, a boat race run around buoys placed in the bay out from the front beach.

Organisation of the Schomberg Cup took place at meetings of the "crew" in the lounge bar at the back of the bar café.. There were protocols, but just about everyone could attend the meetings, which began with the singing of a verse from the *Pirates of Penzance*. The admiral, started the singing with the line, "I am the Admiral of the PPBC" and the crew replied with, "And a right good Admiral too", and so on, similar to the original version. The song always ended with Seagull Sam Wood saying, "and the P is silent as in sea bathing".

All crew members were required to wear the Club badge, a white piece of cloth with yellow letters PPBC inside a propeller. Given the venue, everyone became increasingly argumentative as meetings progressed and rarely was anything agreed.

The crew kept themselves refreshed by calling, "Runner" when their glasses were empty and a junior member would rush to the bar for a refill. On an evening before the Cup race a Calcutta Sweep was held and the competitors were sold at auction.

Staging the race was difficult as all power boats were eligible to compete and the sea had to be calm enough to ensure safety. Race day was frequently cancelled because the sea was considered too rough. Competitors ranged from the Tabarts' *Typhoon*, which was a 30 mph speed boat to small craft powered by 1 hp *Seagulls*. Some of the boats that raced included *Miss Barbara, Atomic, Biljorita, Aunt Spee, Johnny B, Scum & Sweep, Lady Emma, Cutty Sark, Barty (11)* and *Cynic*. The race was handicapped, determined by the time it took all boats to complete one lap of the course. The last boat finishing the one lap trial would start first when the race began. The trouble, however, was there was no way of proving whether every sailor went flat out during the trial lap. In fairness, the handicapper had to disqualify those whose race time was considerably faster than their trial time, a process that resulted in a lot of protests as those involved usually had excuses for the variations.

Sue Graansma remembered "having a simply marvellous time" being allowed to "crew" on one of the boats in the Australia Day boat race.

The club's finale on race day was the Boat Race Ball held in the Mechanic Hall, where the Cup was handed to the winner and Todd Sloane's Band, including Moyle Breton on sax, provided the entertainment.

The Schomberg Cup continued into the late 1950s and in later years has become a golf competition conducted by the Golf Club. Until his death, Wocca Moore was a prominent organiser and traditionally began the announcement of the winner of the golf competition with the singing of the original *Pirates of Penzance* verse.

Off and racing.

The first race meeting of the Port Campbell and District Racing Club was held on Easter Monday, 30 March 1891. The course, which required much preparation, was located outside the township of Port Campbell, towards Peterborough, at the western end of Two Mile Bay. A correspondent from the *Camperdown Chronicle* reported:

> Port Campbell is beginning to take its place in the sporting world. The races held at that place on Easter Monday were a thorough success ... persons who visit the races can, during the intervals, go down the cliffs to the beach, this is worthy of a visit independent of the races.
>
> The course being newly made by the grass trees being cut down, was a little heavy after the rains, but in time it ought to become one of the best country courses in Victoria. Being on the grass tree plains it is fairly level, thus affording spectators a good view of the races from start to finish, and taken altogether is fairly well laid out, being minus of all those sharp turns that seem necessary to most country races. The distance around the course is about six and a half furlongs.
>
> There were six events altogether, which started at 1pm and did not finish until dark. Some dissatisfaction was expressed at the handicapping of the Handicap Trot. It is

said that some maiden trotters were placed on scratch with winners while other maiden trotters were given 40 yards start. For instance a pony of 13 hands and a maiden, was placed on scratch while several upstanding trotters were given 40 yards start, whereas, the pony, to make things equal, should have been placed ahead of these.

Very little money was left at Port Campbell. Two or three trained horses from a distance took nearly all the prizes ... There were two booths on the ground. One was built in a mia-mia fashion, scrub saplings and branches were used in the making of it, giving the place a quite picturesque look. All the growing saplings about had one or two horses tied to each. This in conjunction with the mia-mia, gave the place an amusing aspect.

A ball was subsequently held in the Port Campbell Hall. There was a large attendance, particularly of gentlemen. A few more ladies would have been acceptable to the majority present. Financially the ball was a success as the number of gentlemen more than made up for the ladies.

A century after that first meeting, Marie van Heusden and Anne Radford wrote *A History of the Port Campbell and District Racing Club*, published by Harrison Computer Services, Princetown. The work captured an aspect of the district's social and sporting history for future generations and provided an insight into a different age. While Australians in the late Victorian era had limited opportunities to meet socially and seek recreation, they were clearly keen to do so. "It is not surprising," the authors found, "that the horse, being the primary means of transport, became the focus for sport and entertainment. Not only in the larger towns such as Cobden, Camperdown, Terang, Warrnambool, Portland, Port Fairy, Coleraine were race tracks constructed, but also in the more remote country locations such as Port Campbell, Scotts Creek (Cooreijong Racing Club), Dixie, Princetown (at "Rivernook') and Moonlight Head.

At the Port Campbell races

Ada Cumming riding side-saddle at the races and the Port Campbell Racecourse from the air

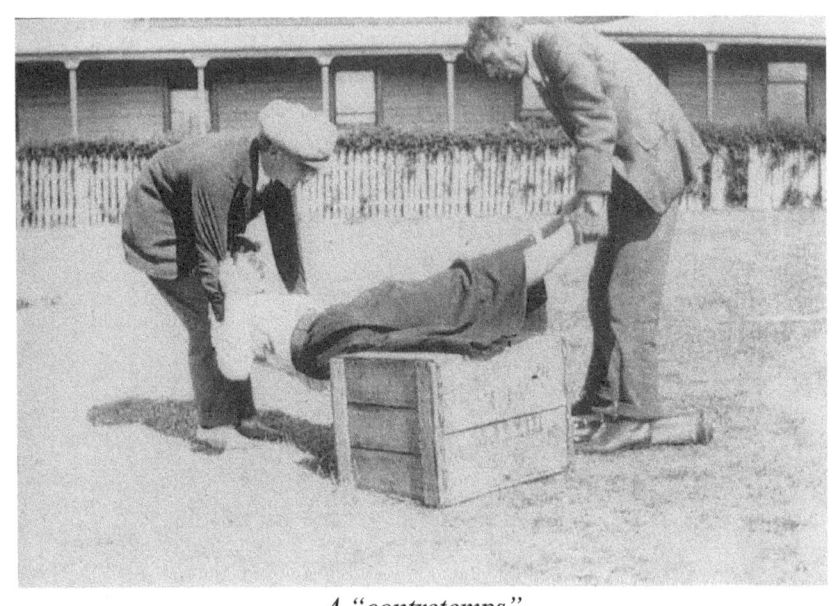

A "contretemps"

Fred Moore, Wocca Moore, Mark Howard

Bill Irvine, Wocca Moore, and Alby Affleck (right)

Roy Officer, Patricia Moore, Moyle Breton and Kit Tinsley

*Senior Officers of the Peterborough Powerboat Club, Des Moore
(1906-85), Tinny Grimwade (1897-1983), Wocca Moore (1918-97),
Andy Chirnside (1906-61), c. 1950*

*Tinny Grimwade, Johnny Bartlam, John Ralston,
crew of 'Alby Affleck, 1949'*

Often the race meetings were followed by a ball which lasted until daybreak when the merry-makers could more easily find their way along bush tracks to their homes."

In the early years, annual race meetings at Port Campbell, followed by a ball and concert, were held just before New Year's Eve, on Easter Mondays, St Patrick's Day or on another date in March.

There were no races at Port Campbell from 1895 to 1901 and from 1917 to 1919. In 1926, the Port Campbell Racing Club affiliated with the Western District Racing Association, later known as the South Western District Racing association. By that year, £60 in prize money was allocated for the seven race meeting, with £18 for the Port Campbell Handicap and £3 for the hack race, a post entry event.

Owen Moore, then aged five, recalled the rooster chase, in which a rooster was let loose for the children to chase with a prize for catching it. He wrote:

> In the 20's we also brought horses with us. My father brought two, Lamardo and Loch Ard and we had Shetland ponies, Tiny and Betty. They came by train to Timboon and were ridden to Peterborough. They were kept in a paddock at the rear of the Hotel yards and sheds; it encompassed the swamp area, its boundaries being the present Robertson/Blair and Mac's Streets which in this day were unmade tracks.

By 1936, as motor cars were becoming the popular mode of transport and fewer families owned horses, interest in horse racing dwindled. The Port Campbell Racing Club felt that by changing the race meetings to a gymkhana, which included a greater variety of events, interest could be rekindled.

The gymkhanas included races for boys and girls, a hundred

yard Open Handicap Foot Race, bowling at the wicket, kicking the football and guessing the live weight of sheep. The horse events included novelty events for hacks and ponies and members of the Light Horse competed in the tent pegging and gave demonstrations. The initial gymkhana was such a success it was repeated in 1937. Van Heusden and Radford noted that members of the Light Horse

> ... looked quite spectacular in their uniforms especially their hats with plumes. Riders and horses would move in unison, walking, running and then trotting. They also demonstrated rescue racing and section fours. The section fours involved one horse jumping the hurdles, then pairs, triples and finally fours, with riders keeping formation.
>
> Members of the Light Horse Brigade were G.V. (Dooley) Worrall, his brother Joe, Jack Currell and Charlie Wilson. The men had very good horses and were obviously excellent horsemen. They travelled around shows entering competitions and won many trophies. One of the trophies is housed in the Port Campbell Historical Society hall.

The gymkhana eventually moved to the Lower Heytesbury Show Grounds and the Port Campbell Race Course was not used again. In 1941 the Committee sold the buildings and fences and invested the £10 raised in war bonds. The club was wound up in 1957 and remaining proceeds donated to the Timboon Hospital (£5) and to the Port Campbell Progress Association (£33) for improvements to the township.

At one race meeting a "bit of a swindle" reportedly took place in a hurdle race. The favourite was known to have a habit of running off the course and missing hurdles. Two jockeys decided to encourage the favourite to go off the course. Some "astute" punters had backed the eventual winner and stood to collect well from a particular bookie. Facing the prospect of going broke, the bookie disappeared and was never seen again.

Van Heusden and Radford also noted that picnic race meetings were held at various places in the district, using temporary fixtures such as a sapling stuck into the ground as a winning post:

> At one meeting at the "Cove" just as the horses were racing down the straight a huge black snake was wriggling his way across the course just near the winning post and what happened? The winning post was pulled from the ground and with it the snake duly dispatched.

Game, set and match

For years, the only tennis court in Peterborough was attached to the south side of the Hotel Annex in Irvine Street. Known as the "Cottage" court it was built by James Irvine 2nd but was not serviceable until Des Moore bought the Annex from John Wiber after the war. Two tennis courts near the Gap were built in about 1951, partly from a £500 donation from Kit Tinsley, who died before they were built. A Tennis Club was established and for many years Lorraine Richmond was the president.

Regular mixed double tennis tournaments have long been a feature of the Australia Day long weekend in Peterborough. This has always been a popular tournament and the two newer public courts on the J.M. Irvine Reserve and the courts at Desmond and Michael Moore's places are used for the tournament.

There were regular tournaments over the Australia Day weekend and at Easter for adults and children. The Final's mixed doubles and winners' presentation has always attracted large crowd. Des Moore's court was used during the summer for regular men's doubles grudge matches.

Bill Cumming wrote this story about his father, Ronald Cumming, the former State MP for Hampden, about a tournament on the "Cottage" tennis court, probably in the 1930s:

Although he was good at most things, my father completely failed to master tennis or golf. I still remember his assault on the tennis court during one Peterborough tennis tournament. Of all people, he drew as his partner Kit Moore, who was a sister of Charlie, Des and Denis, and later married a gentleman by the name of Tinsley. She was also one of the best female players to grace the Peterborough courts.

Kit carried him valiantly through the preliminary rounds, and into the semi-finals, now this was an achievement as it took him two rounds to decide if he was right or left handed. I well remember the final point, my father managed to poke his return of service back over the net, then fell over. Kit played the most unbelievable rally, during which she ran round him, jumped over him, and generally behaved in a most dangerous fashion.

Now and again she would pause to say, "Stay there, Ronald, stay there." He obeyed this command until one of the opponents hit a high lob which, had he stayed there, would have landed on his stomach. The next piece of the action seemed to take place in slow motion – as he rose majestically to his feet the crowd fell silent, and Kit put her head in her hands. He hit it alright, but there are those who say it only bounced once before landing in the Men's Pool.

Note: the Men's Pool was 100 yards away.

Sandcastles and other fun

Other competitions were less formal but every bit as much fun, especially for children. The Sand Castle Competition on the Australia Day weekend was one of the high points of the year for Peterborough children and always produced some amazing

Lady Dumfumblebee, Mayoress of Fumblefun, alias Wocca Moore

structures on the beach. All participants received an Icy Pole and winners are presented to the "Lady Mayoress" and "Lady in Waiting" dressed in drag. The winners are asked to kiss the "Lady Mayoress" (to the chagrin of some of the young boys). This charade has been a feature of the day since the 1940s when Wocca Moore made an especially memorable "Lady Dumfumblebee Mayoress of Fumblefun."

Soos Graansma recalled "the arrival of the Mayoress with an umbrella, wearing a floral creation, a huge bosom, spindly hairy legs, dark glasses, too much lipstick and a tremendous thirst!" Many of Peterborough's younger males have since fulfilled the role and traditionally the Lady Mayoress and Lady in Waiting have to go for a swim in the river in their fine regalia, including hair wigs, high heeled shoes and falsies after the presentation of prizes.

The annual fancy dress ball, originally part of the Peterborough Hotel festivities, has over the years become an eagerly awaited children's event, now held at the Golf Club on Australia Day.

While the sands shift, people and traditions come and go, and Peterborough's robust spirit endures.

Lady Mayoress Dumfumblebee of Fumblefun
(alias Patrick Moore), c. 1990

Epilogue

It's hard now to remember what Peterborough was really like. The endless ocean across Bass Strait – the views across to the Schomberg rock and beyond on a clear day to Moonlight Head, are all still there. But, ah I remember it well!

East of the Curdies River, the Port Campbell Racecourse and the rifle range at Two Mile Bay – gone; the tunnel after the descent down Murray Step and under the Arch collapsed; the steps down to the ledge at Point Hesse inaccessible; London Bridge – collapsed; the beach at London Bridge with its penguin colony blocked off; the Crown of Thorns toppled from its ledge; the spit to the Schomberg Rock – gone.

At the Foreshore Reserve the Pub has gone, first the Café in 1958 and then the Hotel in 1965 – burnt down; the Men's Pool and Giant's Trousers – fenced off; the steps at Shaw's and Ladies Beach are worn away; the log cabin built for the defence of Peterborough in the sand dunes – gone.

West of Peterborough, The Blue Channel steps have worn away; the Sand Slide is devoid of sand; Pirani's Rock inaccessible; Worm Bay without any worms; the Blow Fly huts at Crofts Bay – gone; Densley's hut at Boat Bay – gone. Access to the River at *The Lodge* where there were picnics on windy days, water skiing and fishing has been closed. All these are but memories.

Blowfly huts, Crofts Beach, c. 1950

In old Peterborough township Sturzaker's café, *Tulach Ard*, *Sunny Brae* – the old post office, *Blair Athol* are all gone; *Palmyra* is now a private home as is 'The Cottage'. The Peterborough Power Boat Club is no more, likewise the House of Sin.

Trawling for trout in the Estuary Channel and at the river mouth seems no more. Crayfish are hard to come by especially since "bait sticking" is banned and drop nets have been reduced in size so that the big ones get away with a flip of the tail and the scuba divers and professional potters have taken most of the rest.

Perhaps we can't expect things to have stayed the same, but the coastline is still as beautiful as ever even though the ocean and weather wear it away. The golf course has been improved and the greens are no longer fenced with barbed wire to keep Blair's cows off the greens. Bob Hesketh has for a decade supervised the success of the Peterborough Golf Club with the able assistance of the curator, Hugh Ryan. The Schomberg Cup, once a power boat race on the Bay, is now a golf competition. There are no swimming sports at "The Channel", but there is a path to the Front Beach and steps to Crazy Kate and Worm Bay Beaches for safe swimming. The road to the Bay of Islands has been sealed and car parking and public access improved. The walking track from Crazy Kate to the Bay of Martyrs has been widened and the surface improved. The Tennis Club is continuing the traditional tournaments and the Sandcastle Competition on Australia Day week-end is bigger than ever, albeit the Lady Mayoress and the Lady in Waiting may have altered their fashions somewhat.

The Peterborough Residents Group has been active in planning a new hall on the original Mechanics Hall site next to the Post Office together with a museum. A Residents Group sub-committee has revived interest in the local history. In 2013, the January annual Peterborough Festival was inaugurated with extraordinary success.

There is the Great Ocean Road Tourist Park adjacent to the bridge and a caravan park off MacGillivray Road together with Burl's Hotel Motel which provide accommodation for visitors

The Estuary has masses of black swans and many other birds which nest undisturbed in the "Narrows" entrance to the Curdies River.

Since the 1990s, residential development has extended along the Crazy Kate frontage to the Great Ocean Road. Merrett, MacGillivrays, Casino and Childers Streets to the west and to the north residential development to Antares Street with many more houses. All the residential development has sewerage and water. Peterborough is growing slowly.

The town has a two-truck Fire Station in the Main Street with an active volunteer fire brigade.

In 1964, the Port Campbell National Park was promulgated, extending from Princetown to Peterborough. Later the Bay of Islands Coastal Park was declared, protecting the remnant coastal trees and shrubs from Peterborough to Childer's Cove. Within these two Parks are internationally recognised features such as the Twelve Apostles, Loch Ard Gorge, London Bridge, plus numerous shipwreck sites and the beautiful Bay of Islands. These features will continue to be an attraction, not only to the people of Peterborough, but to those tourists from near and far who traverse the Great Ocean Road all year round.

Bibliography

Shire of Hampden records – information on Daniel Curdie

BOOKS

Charles, Florence & Proctor, Craigie, *Women of the Mount*, Mortlake and District Historical Society, 2009

Charlwood, Don, *Wrecks and Reputations,* Burgewood Books, 3rd edition, 2000

_____ *Settlers Under Sail*, Burgewood Books, 1999

_____ *The 1863 Shipboard Diary of Edward Charlwood*, Burgewood Books, 2003

Dallimore, James, *Journal of the Meek Family History Fellowship*, 1986

Dawson, James, *Australian Aborigines*, Robertson, reprinted 1981

Delaney, Joe, *Delaney's Corner,* Penfolk Publishing, 2004

Doak, Phillip, *Tales from Australia's Shipwreck Coast, A. & F. Doak*, 2002

Duruz, Rosamund, *History of the Curdies River,* Warrnambool Photo-Art Printers, 1976

_____ *Heytesbury Forest Schools*, Ladies' Executive Council of the Timboon Schools 1972

Kiddle, Margaret, *Men of Yesterday,* Melbourne University Press 1963

Loney, Jack, *Old Days and Ways*, Marine History Publications, 1992

_____ *Wrecks Along the Great Ocean Road,* Marine History Publications, 1975

MacKenzie, Jean M. (Bonnie), *My Grandmother's Story*, first published 1986, reprinted 2008

_____ *Sealing, Sailing and Settling in South Western Victoria,* Lowden Publishing 1976

Margaret E. MacKenzie. *Shipwrecks,* National Press, 1964

McAlpine, R.A., *The Shire of Hampden 1863-1963,* Morphet Press, reprinted 1983

Moore, Owen, *Peterborough (As I Remember It) 1924-1939*

O'Callaghan, Elizabeth, *People Who Passed This Way,* Warrnambool and District Historical Society, 2011

Osburne, Richard, *History of Warrnambool from 1847 to 1886,* reprinted 1980

Sayers, C.E., *Of Many Things – A History of Warrnambool Shire,* Olinda Books, 1972

Stevens R. & J., *The Wreck of the* Falls of Halladale *– An Account from the Diary of Jessie Scott MacGillivray Peterborough 1908-1911,* Heytesbury Historical Society, 2009

van Heusen, Marie, & Radford, Anne, *A History of the Port Campbell and District Racing Club*, Harrison Computer Service, Princetown

Weatherly, William, *The Weatherlys of Woolongoon,* Centre for Regional Development, Deakin University, 1998

Wescott, G., Synnot, R., & Powell, M., *Life on the Rocky Shores of S.E. Australia*, Waterwheel Press, 1980

Newspapers and magazines

The Age, 16 July 1877, Letters to the editor

Camperdown Chronicle, 30 March 1891

Curdie, Daniel, "A Journey Through the Scrub", *The Australasian Record,* 17 March 1964

The Warrnambool Examiner, 6 July 1866; 4 May 1869; 9 February 1864; 3 August 1864; 13 December 1864; 1 July 1864; 12 November 1869

The Warrnambool Standard, 14 October 1884; 30 August 1892; 13 January 1899; 16 January 1917; 22 May 1900

Websites

Victorian Heritage database:
  http://vhd.heritage.vic.gov.au/shipwrecks

Information about the Great Ocean Road:
  http://www.greatoceanwalk.info/history-of-the-area/

Cape Otway Lightstation: http://www.lightstation.com

Information on Shipwrecks and diving:
  http://www.flagstaffhill.com/media/uploads/ShipwreckTrail.pdf

  http://www.dpcd.vic.gov.au/heritage/maritime/shipwrecks/
    victorian-shipwreck-dive-sites

  http://www.paradisedivers.com.au/sites/f-halladale.htm

Property records

Old Peterborough township history, SECTION 1

The Old Township was surveyed in 1866 by Nathan Thornley. He divided the area into 6 five acre Sections. Each Section was divided into 10 allotments of 2 roods (half an acre). The sale in fee-simple of 29 lots was for Sections 1,2,3 & 4 (14.5 acres). The upset price was £8 per acre (£4 per lot).

Deposit was 25% of price at sale and balance 30 days

SECTION 1 – 10 lots sold at auction in the Court House, Warrnambool on 5 July1866 for £54. 5s.

This Section is bounded by Mac's & Blair Streets & Schomberg & Halladale Roads. There are a number of significant properties in this Section. Lot 5 was purchased in 1893 by Sarah Macdonald. *Sunny Brae*, the house she built on the Mac's Street frontage became the first post office in Peterborough and a 10 room guest house.

The part of Lot 7 with frontage to Schomberg Road was purchased in the names of Rod Calvert and John Irvine in 1972 for the Peterborough Golf Club although it had been used by the Club for a number of years prior.

No 27 *Cruachan* was once occupied by Mrs Margaret Campbell, wife of Dr Thomas Campbell and former home of Margaret Irvine wife of J.M. (Bill) Irvine and mother of Dr Gerald Irvine and Jenny Porteous.

Corner of Blair Street and Schomberg Road was occupied by Rod and Peg Calvert and children, Alec, Donald and Sally. It was also the first Golf Club House.

No 25 Mac's Street *Nargoort* was the former home of Effie Mackenzie (1863-1961) and Jean (Bonnie) MacKenzie.

J.M. (Bonnie) MacKenzie was the author of *My Grandmother's*

Story; Sealing, Sailing and Settling in South Western Victoria; Shipwrecks and More Shipwrecks (in collaboration with her mother Effie MacKenzie) and the *Peacock from the Sea.*

Allotment 1   Vol 3353/501 – 2 Roods

Title Date

1866 William Kuck of Warrnambool paid £4.7s

1921 Stephen Bailey of Derrinallum

1923 Caroline Bailey

1947 Thomas Cook – skinbuyer – died 1965

1951 SUBDIVIDED – 3 LOTS

Corner – Lot 1 Vol 8653/320

Robert Cook & Ben Cook (died 1995)

1973 Robert Cook & Dorothy Taylor (died 1982)

1982 Alice Cook

1985 Clement Meade

1985 Clement & Faye Meade

1990 Frances & Wendy O'Connor

Lot 2 – Schomberg Road Vol 8653/321

1967 Robert & Ben Cook (died 1950

1995 Ben Cook & Della Bishop

1995 John & Aileen Pekin

Lot 3 – Halladale Road Vol 7640/107

1952 Michael O'Donahue (died 1965)

1966 James O'Donahue

Allotment 2   Vol 240/913

1866 Robert Scott paid £4.15s

1892 Margaret Scott

1909 Margaret MacKenzie

1947 John Noonan

1959 Marie Milroy, Dawn Gelant, John Noonan, Agnes Nugent,
Bernard Noonan

Allotment 3   Vol 2124/639

1866 Thomas Asche paid £5 (noted land shark – see transcript
reference)

1905 Minnie Callaway

1908 Sarah Macdonald

1934 Margaret MacKenzie (Tulach Ard), Sarah Milne & Mary
Nieman

1936 Jean MacKenzie

1936 SUBDIVIDED – 2 LOTS

Mac's Street Lot Vol 7596/149

1935 Claire Hayes

1969 Henry Wilkinson

1974 John & Catherine Noonan

1996 John, Catherine & Denis Noonan & Christine Spong

Schomberg Road Lot Vol 7890/128

1953 James Boydle

1963 Judy Chirnside

Allotment 4 Vol 220/871

1866 James Mayon paid £5

1988 Barry Jenkins Vol/Fol 9824/839

SUBDIVIDED

1988 Mac's Street Lot Barrie Jenkins Vol 9828/877

1989 Schomberg Road Lot Peter & Audrey Deppeler Vol 9828/878

Allotment 5   Vol 443/454

1893 Bucharest & Young paid £4

1893 Andrew Tobil

1893 Thomas Merrett of Mepunga, Grazier

1893 Sarah Macdonald

1935 Margaret MacKenzie

SUBDIVIDED

Schomberg Road Lot Vol 6471/019

1941 Hilda Anderson

1948 Alan Saber

1951 Michael O'Donahue

1964 Albert & Barbara Nash

1980 Robert & Jonathan Nash

1980 Robert & Joan Nash

1983 Robert & Frances Loader

Mac's Street Lot Vol 8094/952

1953 Bessie MacKenzie

1964 Hugh & Veronica Ryan

1998 Hugh Ryan

Allotment 6 Vol 282/564

1866 Llewellyn Evans paid £4

1908 Minnie Callaway

1910 Sarah Macdonald (died 1934)

1917 Jessie MacGillivray (died 1934)

1935 Margaret Nieman

SUBDIVIDED

Mac's Street Lot Vol 8424/967

1935 Margaret Allen (died 1962)

1963 Nora Lawson (died 1999), Kathleen Allen(died 1955) & Nancy Allen (died 1989) equal shares

1985 Nancy Allen (Kathleen's share)

1989 Nora Lawson – Nancy Allen's share

1989 Ron Cashin, Hugo Goetze, John Fletcher – (two thirds share)

1999 Christopher & Caroline Goetze – one-third share

1999 Margaret Goetze – one third share

Schomberg Road Lot Vol 7425/967

1953 Stan Brown (died 1985) & Edna Brown

1986 Edna Brown, John Brown & Marilyn Reid

Allotment 7 Vol 197/376

1866 Duncan Walker paid £4.4s

1890 Margaret Walker & William Walker

1908 Minnie Callaway

1909 Sarah Macdonald

1935 Sarah Milne

SUBDIVIDED

Mac' Street Lot Vol 8432/173

1936 Margaret Campbell

1963 Wilma Collie

Schomberg Road Lot 7611/118

1950 George Richards

1960 Stan Brown

1961 William Armstrong

1972 N.R. Calvert & J.S. Irvine

1976 J.S. Irvine & Peter Clark

1990 Peterborough Golf Club

Allotment 8   Vol 674/670

1866 Thomas Smith paid £6.13s

1880 Mary Pallas

1882 David Kelson

1906 Minnie Callaway

1910 Sarah Macdonald

1921 Stephen Bailey

1923 Else Bailey

1947 Margaret Calvert (Peg)

Allotment 9   Vol 674/671

1866 Thomas Smith £7.15s

1881 Mary Pallas

1882 David Kelson

1906 Minnie Callaway

1911 Sarah Macdonald

1921 Stephen Bailey

1922 William Bailey

1948 Margaret MacKenzie

SUBDIVIDED

Corner Lot Vol 7639/182

1949 Ken Row

1969 Robin Bowden

Mac's Street Lot Vol 7324/614

1948 Jean MacKenzie (died 1990)

1990 Kathryn Wilkinson

Allotment 10   Vol 674/672

1866 Thomas Smith paid £8.11s

1881 Mary Pallas

1906 Minnie Callaway

1907 Charles MacGillivray & Tom McKenzie

1937 Margaret MacKenzie

SUBDIVIDED

Mac's Street Lot

1951 Keith McKenzie & Berdie MacKenzie Vol 7692/172

1956 Elizabeth MacKenzie

1964 Muriel Collie

1974 A & D Reid

1974 William & Heather Wood

Corner Lot Vol 7800/076

1952 Ian & Elizabeth MacKenzie

1964 Muriel Collie (died 1972)

1974 Alan & Doreen Wood

1976 Janet Parlour

Old Peterborough township history – SECTION 2

Lot 1-5 & 10 were sold at the 11am Warrnambool Court House auction on 5 July 1866. Thomas Merrett bought the remainder in 1873.

The Crown received a total of £55.1s for the 10 allotments

Significant properties

Lot 10 purchased in 1915 by the Crown became the Mechanic's Institute – Peterborough Public Hall built in 1918.

Lot 2 Mac's Street frontage. For many years it was the post office, store and home of Ken and Aila Row(daughter of Tom McKenzie).

Lot 3 Mac's Street frontage – site of guest house *Tulach Ard*, later *Doo Drop Inn*, it was destroyed by fire in 1967. The site was purchased by

Effie MacKenzie in 1907. *Tulach Ard* had also served as the Tom MacKenzie family home.

Lot 5 Schomberg Road frontage – purchased in 1937 by Andrew Chirnside who built *Karrawingie*, a two story architect designed house was built in 1950. Andrew Chirnside was a grazier from *Moorallah* , near Skipton.

Lot 9 was purchased from the Crown by Thomas Merrett in 1873 for £7.15s and is the site of Hamilton's Cottage built on the corner of Irvine Road & Mac's Street by Margaret Hamilton in 1877. From 1908, when purchased by James Irvine, it was used as an annex to the Hotel, until changed to the family holiday home of Desmond Moore in 1951. Substantial renovations were then supervised by Melbourne architect, Geoffrey Sommers. The main part of the original cottage is still substantially in its original state.

Allotment 1 Vol 240/953

1866 J. Davies of Warrnambool £7.2s

1871 Charles Stewart Affleck of Curdies Inlet, Heytesbury 391/145

1909 Daniel Wilkie

1916 Samuel Mann, Caramut, grazier (from *Lawrenny* purchased 1904)

1937 Eustace Cockrill

SUBDIVIDED

Corner Lot Vol 7208/463

1948 Lorna Ethel Bartlam

1984 Frances & Margaret Carlin

Schomberg Road Lot Vol116/029

1939 Thomas Atkins

1944 Marlene Atkins

1959 John Malcolm & Jennifer Louise Seccull

1961 Deborah Cunliffe

1965 Virginia Mercer ("Bardie")

Allotment 2 Vol 952/206 original title unavailable

1866 Thomas Merrett

1875 Jemima Robertson (widow from *Connewarren*, Mortlake)

1890 Alexander Robertson

1894 Helen Blair

1907 Margaret MacKenzie Vol 2557/225

1944 Aileen & Kenneth Row Vol 6750/824

1955 Colin Vagg Vol 8105/041

1988 Keith, Elizabeth & Arthur Morarty

1992 K & E Morarty

1993 Geoffrey & Marlene Couch

Allotment 3 Vol 198/573

1866 Nathan Thornley £5.1s

1878 Jemima Robertson Vol 1012/308

1890 Alexander Robertson

1894 Helen Blair

1907 Margaret MacKenzie – Tulach Ard

1955 Keith McKenzie, son of Tom Mckenzie, affectionately
      known as "Skimmy"

SUBDIVIDED

Schomberg Road Lot Vol 8104/945

1965 Jane Gilder

1981 Susan Philip

1983 C.Rosemary Durham

Mac's Street Lot

1966 Malvery Gladman

1968 Duncan McNab & C. R Crozier-Durham Unit 1 Vol 9781/565,
      Unit 2 Vol 9781/566

1988 D McNab Unit 1

1988 C.R. Crozier-Durham Unit 2

1988 McGennan Nominees Pty Ltd Unit 2

Allotment 4 Vol 443/455

1866 Bucharest £4

1890 Margaret Hamilton

1897 Andrew & Mary Hamilton Consolidated lots 4,5, 6,7,8, & 9

1897 Mary Hamilton Vol 2644/677

1908 James Irvine Vol 528/677

1919 Ester Irvine & James George Irvine Vol 6083/438

SUBDIVIDED

Schomberg Road Lot

1955 Ruth Grimwade

1956 Virginia Mercer

1968 Deborah Cunliffe

Mac's Street Lot

1938 James George Irvine

1952 Bryan Austin

1957 Harold Austin

1964 Susan Philip

Allotment 5 Vol 190/888

1866 J. Bucharest £5

1890 Margaret Hamilton

1897 Andrew & Mary Hamilton

1897 Mary Hamilton

1908 James Irvine

1919 Ester & James George Irvine

1938 James George Irvine

SUBDIVIDED

Schomberg Road Lot Vol 8531/271

1937 Andrew Chirnside

1952 Elsa Chirnside

1964 Percy & Edna Stafford

1990 Percy Stafford

1994 Max & Margaret Magilton

2000 Derek & Felicity Magilton
          Mac's Street Lot Vol 7917/099

1952 Ann Judy Austin

Allotment 6 Vol 644/681

1873 T. Merrett £4

1875 Margaret Hamilton

1890 Andrew & Mary Hamilton

1897 Mary Hamilton

1908 James Irvine

1919 Ester & James George Irvine

1938 James George Irvine

SUBDIVIDED

Schomberg Road Lot

1949 Andrew Chirnside

1952 Elsa Chirnside

1964 Percy and Edna Stafford

1990 P. Stafford

1994 Max and Margaret Magilton

2000 D. & F. Magilton

Mac's Street Lot

1949 John & Theresa Jenkins

1954 June Sturzaker & Charles Merrett Vol 8063/535

John and Theresa Jenkins built a café on this site, later operated by June Sturzaker. In 1956 it was burnt down.

1959 Ben & Beryl Fowler

1961 Herbert Eales

1962 Ian & Gary Smith

1967 James Dowling Wilson

Allotment 7 Vol 644/681

1873 T Merrett £4.4s

1875 Margaret Hamilton

1890 Andrew & Mary Hamilton

1897 Mary Hamilton

1908 James Irvine

1919 Ester Irvine & James George Irvine

1938 James George Irvine

1943 Mary Weibye

SUBDIVIDED

Schomberg Road Lot

1949 Ava Lorraine Richmond
Mac's Street Lot

1953 F.W. Coy 8053/072 – Frank and Jean Coy

1958 Jean Coy

1989 Peter Coy

Allotment 8 Vol 644/683

1873 T. Merrett £6.13 s

1875 Margaret Hamilton

1890 Andrew & Mary Hamilton

1897 Mary Hamilton

1908 James Irvine

1919 Ester Irvine & James George Irvine

1938 James George Irvine

1938 Edith Mary Moore (Peterborough – manager) Vol 6259/753

1950 Margaret Murphy of Timboon

1950 L. Tabart & E.J. Joyce Vol 7419/764

SUBDIVIDED

Schomber Road Lot

1950 A.W. Moore

1996 June Moore

Corner Lot Vol 8143/830

1956 L. & M. Tabart

1961 Mafe Tabart

Lyn and Mafe Tabart built the house here after spending many years camping in a caravan on the foreshore nearby.

1992 G. & P. Loving

Irvine Road Lot Vol 8143/829

1956 E.J. Joyce – Jan Joyce

1983 J.R. Joyce & S. Graansma

Allotment 9 Vol 694/684

1873 T. Merrett £7.15s

1875 Margaret Hamilton

1897 Andrew & Mary Hamilton

1897 Mary Hamilton

1908 James Irvine

1919 Ester Irvine & James George Irvine

1938 James George Irvine

1943 Mary Weibye

1951 Desmond C. Moore

1983 E.R. Moore

1998 M. Coldham & C. Morrison

Allotment 10 Vol 189/624

1866 Richard Harrington £8.6s

1882 Jemima Robertson

1890 Alexander Robertson

1894 Helen Blair

1915 Crown – Mechanics Hall built here in 1918

Old Peterborough township history – SECTION 3

Lots 1-4 were sold at the auction on 5 July 1866 – Warrnambool Court House. Upset price £8/acre, except lot 3, £12/acre.

This Section of land, bounded by Irvine, Mac's, Blair & Robertson Streets, became the focal point of Peterborough with the development in 1885 of *Peterborough House* as a guest house on the corner of Mac's and Irvine Streets. James Irvine purchased all of this Section between 1891 and 1916 with the exception of Lot 2. Lot 2 is the lot purchased in the name of John Thomas Meek at the Warrnambool auction in 1866. James Irvine was drowned crossing the river in 1919. His body was never found.

The Inscription on the James Irvine memorial says:

Erected by residents and visitors to Peterborough in affectionate memory of James Irvine who lost his life crossing the Curdies River 24 June 1919.

The guest house became the *Peterborough* Hotel in 1903. The land to the west was used for servicing the Hotel. The rear paddock was used for grazing milking cows and horses for the guests with a flock of geese on the swamp. The Hotel was destroyed by fire in 1965, ending a significant era in Peterborough's history.

In 1981 the Prime Minister of Australia, John Malcolm Fraser built a holiday home on Lot 14 in Robertson Street. Fraser and his family occupied this property until 1996.

Allotment 1 Vol 189/622

1866 William Hamilton of Mortlake paid £7

1873 Thomas Shaw

1891 James Irvine

1919 James George Irvine & Esther Irvine

1938 James George Irvine

1943 Mary Weibye

1947 John & Ruby Wiber

1948 John Wiber 8223/435

PART OF 15 LOT SUBDIVISION

Allotment 2 Vol 196/133 Corner Robertson & Irvine Streets

It is probable that James Meek purchased this lot and put the title in the name of his son, John because of his precarious financial situation.

1866 John Thomas Meek paid £6, the upset price for a half acre

James Meek built a cottage and dug a well on this site around 1854/5. He returned to Warrnambool in 1856, but came back to Peterborough intermittently.

Note: Nathan Thornley did not complete his Peterborough survey until 1865

Meek's cottage was probably the first dwelling built in Peterborough and was probably in sight of the shipwrecked "Schomberg" on Boxing Day 1855.

1901 Robert Blair

1920 William Blair

1921 James Robertson (died 1923)

1924 William Armstrong

1925 Adeline Catherine Cumming, "Mt Fyans" Camperdown

1950 Ada Doris Winter-Irving 7444/733(sister of W.R Cumming)

The house on this property was called "Moonya".

SUBDIVIDED

Vol 8261/209 Irvine Street

1960 Frank Stephens

1967 Stanley Turnbull

1976 Joyce Turnbull

1997 Rosalind Wallis

Vol 8329/495 Corner Irvine & Robertson Streets

1961 Stanley Turnbull

1976 Joyce Turnbull

1996 William Turnbull

Allotment 3 Vol 291/185

1866 Martin Conway paid £10.1 – valued @ £40

It is possible that James Meek's hut and well were erected on this lot because there were improvements valued at £40 and the Upset Price (reserve) was £12 per acre or £6 for the half acre block and it sold for £10.1s.

1889 G. & A. Freeman

1894 James Irvine

1919 James George Irvine & Esther Irvine

1938 James George Irvine

1943 Mary Weibye

1947 John & Ruby Wiber

1948 John Wiber

PART OF 15 LOT SUBDIVISION

Allotment 4 Vol 189/621

1866 William Hamilton of Mortlake paid£13

1873 Thomas Shaw 631/041

1891 James Irvine

1919 James George Irvine & Esther Irvine

1938 James George Irvine

1943 Mary Weibye

1947 John & Ruby Wiber

1948 John Wiber

PART OF 15 LOT SUBDIVISION

Allotment 5 Vol 3958/475

1916 James Irvine paid £52

1919 James George Irvine & Esther Irvine

1938 James George Irvine

1943 Mary Weibye

1947 John & Ruby Wiber

1948 John Wiber

Allotments 6, 7 & 8 Vol 2768/450

1899 James Irvine paid £25

1920 James George Irvine & Esther Irvine

1938 James George Irvine

1943 Mary Weibye

1947 John & Ruby Wiber

1948 John Wiber

Lot 1 Vol 8223/435 Corner Mac's & Irvine, 1 acre 32 perches

1958 Peterborough Hotel Pty Ltd Purchased Lots 1, 5, 6, 8, 9, 10, 11, 12, 13, 14,15

1966 Barry Jenkins & Mary Andrews Vol 8892/059

1968 Peterborough Motor Inn Pty Ltd

Lot 2 Vol 8187/452 Mac's Street

1958 B. & M. Murray

1960 Betsy Tehan

2000 Keith & Neil Harvey * Frances Sticpenict

2000 Beryl Harvey

Lot 3 Vol 8157/643 Mac's Street

1955 Helen McCulloch

Lot 4 Vol 8157/643

1957 Judy Howard

1995 Lorraine, Indi & Edward Richardson

Lots 5 & 6 Vol 8435/919 Mac's Street

1963 John & Jean Edwards Vol 8469/565 & 566

1975 John & Patrick Ryan

1977 William & Patricia Burl

1991 K. & E. Morarty

1993 Charis Pelling

1998 Lynette Atkinson & Kathleen Burl

2000 Kathleen Burl

Lot 7 Vol 7797/ 009 Mac's Street

1952 Richard Coy (died 1990)

1991 Bryoney Hallowes

Lots 8 & 9 Vol 8397/235 Corner Robertson & Blair Streets

1962 Mavis Smith

1987 Charis Pelling

2000 Michael & Pamela Foley

Lots 10 & 11 Vol 8780/985 Robertson Street

1961 Florence Calvert

2000 Keith Calvert

Lot 12 Vol 8892/059 Robertson Street

1971 S.J. Wilson

Lot 13 Vol 8744/379 Robertson Street

1968 Timothy Gillespie

Lot 15 Vol 8589/945 Robertson Street

1965 J. & J. Turnbull

1980 Joyce Turnbull

1980 James Turnbull

Lot 14 Vol 8744/380 Robertson Street

1968 Nancy Stephens

1976 Mary Moore

1981 John Malcolm Fraser (former Prime Minister of Australia)

1988 Neeran Nominees Pty Ltd

1996 Justin & Julie McNab

Old Peterborough township history – SECTION 4

This Section is bounded by Blair, Mac's & Robertson Streets and the unmade Halladale Road on the west side. All allotments were sold in 1866 for a total of £77.4s.

Significant properties in this Section include:

Lot 8 purchased by Annette Breton in 1926. Annette lived there until her death in 1967 and her son Moyle until his death in 1987.

Lot 9 is the site of *The Big House* built by Jemima Robertson in about 1874. It was used as a guest house became the *Blair Athol* after the purchase by Helen Blair in 1894. After Helen Blair died in 1926, the business was continued by her two daughters Lily Ann and Mary Jane. Lily died in 1948 and Mary in 1956. The property was sold by Lex and Nancy Blair in 1957 ending a long connection in Peterborough with the Helen Blair family.

Lot 1 Vol 679/673

1866 Thomas Smith of Dennington paid £7.4s

1881 Mary Pallas Vol 1232/400

1882 David Kelson

1906 Minnie Callaway

1907 Charles MacGillivray (died 1915) & Tom MacKenzie Vol 4340/899

1935 Margaret MacKenzie

1936 Jessie Nieman

1937 Gertrude Thomas

SUBDIVIDED

Mac's Street

1952 George & Bonnie Burns Vol 7749/127

1954 Violet Watson Vol 8071/328

1954 Margaret Francis (died 1975)

1977 Keith & Elanor Hughes

1980 Andrew & Mary Gubbins

Lot 2 674/674

1866 Thomas Smith (died 1880) paid £6.5s

1881 Mary Pallas

1882 David Kelson

1906 Minnie Callaway Vol 3240/899

1907 Charles MacGillivray & Tom McKenzie

1935 Margaret MacKenzie, Sarah Milne & Mary Nieman

1935 Margaret MacKenzie

Lot 3

1866 Thomas Smith paid £7.3s

1881 Mary Pallas Vol 1232/400

1882 David Kelson of Warrnambool

1906 Minnie Callaway of Timboon

1907 Charles MacGllivray & Tom McKenzie Vol 3240/899

1935 Margaret MacKenzie, Sarah Milne & Mary Nieman

1936 Margaret MacKenzie

Lot 4 Vol 192/388

1866 Andrew McWilliam of Terang paid £8.6s

1877 Jemima Robertson

1890 Alexander Robertson

1894 Helen Blair

1930 Lily Ann & Mary Jane Blair

SUBDIVIDED

Robertson Street Lot

1958 Mary Andrew 8619/127

1966 Robert Richardson

1976 Judith & Keith Armstrong half share Vol 9181/548

1976 Judith Armstrong – half share Vol 9181/549

Mac's Street Part

1921 Donald McDonald

1946 George Gill

1948 George Gill & Francis Roddy Vol 7188/421

1951 Lawrence Murnane Vol 7670/077

1961 Jean Murnane

1983 Kathryn Heffernan, Robyn Murfett & Michael Murnane Vol
      8154/385

Lot 5 Vol 663/481

1866 W Dickinson paid £7.6s

1877 Jemima Robertson

1890 Alexander Robertson

1894 Helen Blair Vol 2557/225

1930 Lily Ann (died 1948) & Mary Jane Blair Vol 5652/216

1950 Mary Jane Blair (died 1956)

SUBDIVIDED

Robertson Street Lot

1956 Ruth Blair

1958 Mary Andrew

1958 Nan de Crespigney

Lot 6 Vol 652/268 – 2 roods

1866 David Angus

1877 Jemima Robertson

1890 Alexander Robertson

1894 Helen Blair

1930 Lily Ann & Mary Jane Blair

SUBDIVIDED

Mac's Street Lot

1952 George Richards

1965 Ruby & Margaret Yeoman

1976 Robert & Dawn Case

Robertson Street Lot

1957 Alex & Nancy Blair & Elizabeth Welton

1984 Island Bay Pty Ltd

1992 Margaret Irvine

Lot 7 Vol 189/638

1866 S. McGregor

1877 Jemima Robertson

1890 Alexander Robertson

1894 Helen Blair

1930 Lily Ann & Mary Jane Blair

SUBDIVIDED

Mac's Street Lot

1948 Annette Breton (died 1967)

1967 T.M. Breton

1970 Alan Thomas

1978 Robert & Dawn Case

Robertson Street Lot

1957 Alex & Nancy Blair & Elizabeth Welton

1971 John, Odette, Yvonne, & John McKie

1986 Odette & John McKie

1996 John McKie

1996 Ken & Maria Murfett

Lot 8 Vol 189/618

1866 Frederick Charles Flaxman paid £7.9s

1877 Jemima Robertson

1890 Alexander Robertson

1894 Helen Blair

SUBDIVIDED

Corner Lot

1926 Annette Breton

1967 Trowell Moyle Breton (died 1987)

1987 J.W. Barrett

1999 Bernadette Price

Blair Street Part

1951 Alex & Nancy Blair

1973 Maurice Davidson & Maureen Steel

2000 Maureen Steel

Lot 9 Vol 189/644

1866 S. McGregor paid £6

1877 Jemima Robertson

1890 Alexander Robertson Vol 2557/225

1931 Lily Ann & Mary Jane Blair

1946 Leslie Keane Vol 6870/941

1957 Alex & Nancy Blair

SUBDIVIDED

Blair Street Lot 1

1960 Jane Tinsley

1965 Jane & Michael Tinsley

1977 Jane Gilder

Corner Lot 2

1960 Peter Bury

1962 Margaret Kelly

1976 Jane Gilder

Lot 10 Vol 291/184

1866 Martin Conway paid £9.1s

1898 Sarah Conway

1902 Charles Callaway

1907 Charles MacGillivray & Tom McKenzie

1926 Tom Mckenzie

1947 Richard & Caroline Carty Vol 9176/739

1976 Keith & Barbara Reid

SUBDIVIDED

Lot 2 Vol 9461/639 Robertson Street

1982 W.D & P McCulloch

1986 Nan De Crespigney

Lots 1 & 3 9461 638 & 6640 Corner Robertson Street & Halladale Road

1990 Thomas Ward

1993 Ileola Pty Ltd

1998 Graham & Heather Murfett

Old Peterborough township history – SECTION 5

Lot 1 Vol 644/673

1876 Jemima Robertson

1894 Helen Blair

1930 Lily Ann & Mary Jane Blair

1950 Mary Jane Blair

Lot 2 Vol 644/674

1876 Jemima Robertson

1894 Helen Blair

1930 Lily Ann & Mary Jane Blair

1950 Mary Jane Blair

Lot 3 Vol 644/690

1873 Adam Mackay

1889 Alexander Robertson

1894 Helen Blair

1930 Lily Ann & Mary Jane Blair

1950 Mary Jane Blair

Lot 4 Vol 644/675

1876 Jemima Robertson

1894 Helen Blair

1930 Lily Ann & Mary Jane Blair

1950 Mary Jane Blair

Lot 5 Vol 644/676

1873 W. Lock of Mepunga paid £6

1876 Jemima Robertson

1894 Helen Blair

1930 Lily Ann & Mary Jane Blair

1950 Mary Jane Blair

Lot 6 Vol 644/691

1873 Adam Mackay of Warrnambool paid £6

1889 Mary Mackay

1889 Alexander Robertson

1894 Helen Blair

1930 Lily Ann & Mary Jane Blair

1950 Mary Jane Blair

Lot 7 Vol 644/677

1873 W. Lock paid £4

1876 Jemima Robertson

1894 Helen Blair

1930 Lily Ann & Mary Jane Blair

1950 Mary Jane Blair

Lot 8 Vol 8274/280

1956 Ruth Victoria Blair

Lot 9 Vol 644/678

1873 W.H. Lock paid £7

1876 Jemima Robertson Vol 872/283

1890 Alexander Robertson

1894 Helen Blair

1947 Leslie Keane

1953 Ila Bartlett

SUBDIVIDED

Lot 1Vol 8907/621

1971 Ila Bartlett

1971 James & Alice Kelly

Lot 2 Vol 8907/623

1971 Ila Bartlett

Lot 10 Vol 644/692

1873 Bruce Mackay (died 1884) paid £8

1885 Mary Mackay

1889 Alexander Robertson

1894 Helen Blair

Old Peterborough township history – SECTION 6

Significant properties in this Section are:

Lot 1, purchased by Ruth Blair in 1917 it was for many years the "Palmyra" guest house and had been used as a "subsidised" school.

Lots 5 & 6 were purchased by Alby and Gwen Affleck in 1914. Daughter, Gwen Kelly was a sister to Ruth Grimwade. Her house on Lot 6 in Robertson Street later became known as the *House of Sin* when occupied by Will Kelly and his friends.

William Ronald Cumming moved the house *Falls of Halladale* onto the Hamilton Street frontage of Lot 5 & 6 in about 1942. Opposite this house in Hamilton Street and next to the Schomberg Motel was

Moness, the former home of James George Irvine (1879-1965) and his wife Isabella. The house was demolished in about 2007.

Lots 7, 8 & 9 were the site of the first Presbyterian Church built in 1885. This wooden structure was replaced in 1934 by the brick church now used as a home by W. Saunders. The land was donated to the Presbyterian Church by Jemima Robertson.

Lot 1 Vol 217/252

1867 Lee from Koroit paid £5

1909 Tait

1909 William Blair

1910 John Horne, John Stock, Denis Clark & William Baxter

1917 Ruth Victoria Blair (died 1961) Vol 8538/078

1965 James Boydle

1975 John Boydle

Lot 2 Vol 217/258

1867 Samuel McGregor paid £4

Vesting order to E.Tucker & E Chapple Vol 8133/194, Vol 8179/215 & 216

1957 James George Irvine

SUBDIVIDED

Robertson Street Lot

1957 Fred Moore

1959 Florence Calvert

Hamilton Street Lot

1951 Joan Cumming Vol 8885/048

1991 Susan Cumming

Lot 3 Vol 217/249

1887 James Dickson paid £4

1907 John Gerald Irvine

1921 Esther & James George Irvine

1938 James George Irvine

SUBDIVIDED

Robertson Street lot

1955 Fred Moore Vol 8091/698 Fred Moore was the former Managing
Director of Charles Moore Ltd department store retailers.

Hamilton Street Lot Vol 8303/150

1960 Owen Moore

1965 Owen & Mary Moore

1999 Owen Moore

Lot 4 Vol 217/248

1887 James Dickson of Warrnambool paid £4

1907 John Gerald Irvine

1921 Esther & James Irvine Vol 4459/783

1938 James George Irvine

SUBDIVIDED

Robertson Street Lot

1955 Fred Moore

Hamilton Street Lot

1960 Jan Rogers

Lot 5 Vol 2327/314

1889 Robert Blair paid £16

1916 Gwen Affleck of *Minjah*, Hawkesdale

1925 Ava Cumming (died 1940, first wife of W.R Cumming)

1942 William Ronald Cumming (died 1951)

1954 Nora Cumming (second wife of W R Cumming)

1951 Lindsay Morrison

SUBDIVIDED Vol 9541/847

1958 Leslie Clarke

1983 Barry & Robert Clarke

1988 Barry Clarke

1997 Michael & Carmel Kavanagh

Robertson Street Lot

No title available

Lot 6 Vol 2230/863

1889 Charles Jones Mounted Constable of Port Campbell paid £16

1909 William Blair

1910 Minnie Callaway

1913 Samuel Dunlop of Terang

1916 Gwen Affleck

1925 Ava Cumming Vol 5067/393 1964 8595/703 (first wife of W.R Cumming)

1942 William Ronald Cumming

1951 L.R.Morrison

SUBDIVIDED

1988 Barry Clarke

1997 M. & C. Kavanagh

Lot 7 Vol 5717/288

1930 No original title – Act of State Parliament No 391, 24 December 1930 gives powers of disposition for lots 7, 8 & 9 to the Presbyterian Church.

1933 Presbyterian Church

1933 Weeks Vol 5850/977

SUBDIVIDED

Robertson Street Lot

1971 W. Saunders

Hamilton Street Lot

1979 Myrtle Clarke

1983 Barry & Robert Clarke

1988 Barry Clarke.

1997 M. & C. Kavanagh

Lot 8 Vol 5717/288

1930 No title original title available – Act of Parliament gives
        property rights to Presbyterian Church

1933 Presbyterian Church Vol 5717/288

1933 Eunice Wood

1933 Jessie Scott

1940 Charles Lindquist (died 1962)

SUBDIVIDED 3 LOTS

1963 Wilfred Weigall

Robertson Street lot

1972 William & Pat Burl

1997 Pat Burl

Irvine Street Lot

1969 Violet Keane

1973 Edward Gray

1973 Lindsay Morrison

1987 Lydia Sinclair

Corner Lot

1969 Violet Keane

1973 Edward Gray

1973 Lindsay Morrison

1990 Frank & Margery Nicholsen

1999 Damien & Lee Ann O'Neill

Lot 9 Vol 5717/288

1930 No title. Act of Parliament gives property rights to Presbyterian church

1971 W. Saunders Vol 9389/236 & Vol 9389/235

Lot 10 Vol 217/247

1867 J. Dickson paid £5

1907 John Irvine

1910 Ester Irvine

1921 Ester & James George Irvine Vol 4459/783 Section 6 Lots 3, 4 & 10

1938 James George Irvine

SUBDIVIDED

Corner Lot Vol 8177/534

1958 Margaret Kelly (died 1991)

1992 Eve Greig

1994 Paul, Pat & Brendan Kelly

Little Peterborough and North Hamilton Street

Titles Office Information

This area was originally surveyed as 32 allotments

Lot 1 – Corner Antares & Peterborough Road Vol 3440/963

1907 Joseph Ballis paid £10 for 2.5 acres

1925 Ruth Blair

1962 Barry Jenkins

Subdivided in LP 62359 – 13 Lots west of Newfield Street

LP110216 – 12 lots east side of Newfield Street

Lot 2 – Vol 3507/309

1907 Joseph Ballas paid £8.10s for 1.75 acres

1925 Ruth Blair

1962 Barry Jenkins

Subdivided

Lot 3 – South of Lots 1 & 2

1907 Charles MacGillivray (Peterborough grazier) paid £4for 1.5
       acres

1935 Margaret MacKenzie, Sarah Milne & Mary Nieman Vol
       5990/924

1936 Sarah Milne Vol 6084/691

1941 T.M. Breton

1947 Albert Payne

Subdivided LP34929 – 6 lots

Lot 4

1907 Charles MacGillivray (Peterborough grazier) paid £4 for 1.5
       acres

1935 Margaret MacKenzie, Sarah Milne, Mary Nieman

1936 Norman Nieman Vol 6084/692

1941 T.M. Breton

1947 Albert Payne

1950 Leonard Payne (died 1987)

1989 Edward Payne

Lot 5 – Corner Champion Street & Peterborough Road

1906 Sarah Sorlie Macdonald paid £3

1907 1935 Norman MacGillivray Nieman

1941 T.M. Breton (Postal Officer)

1947 Albert Payne

1950 Lynden Linaker Vol 7591/116

1987 Maureen Bain

1993 Jerry & Christine Page

Lot 6 – South Corner Champion Street & Peterborough Road

1892 William Irwin paid £5 1/8 for 1.25 acres

1953 J.M. & J.S. Irvine Vol 9570/773 consolidated lots 6,7,8 & 9

1984 Thomas & Ellen Scouller subdivided Vol 9615/654& 655 & 656

SUBDIVIDED

Vol 9615/654 – 2 lots

1989 Lambert Vol 9884/926

Vol 9884/927 Schouller

Vol 9615/655 – 2 lots

1991 Scouller Vol 9912/419

1991 K. & V. Murfitt Vol 9912/420

Lot 7

1893 William Irwin paid £5 5/2 for 1.25 acres

1900 Thomas Burt

1908 Charles MacGillivray

1909 Margaret McDonald

1919 Thomas Shaw

1924 Arthur Keith Urquhart

1953 J.M. & J.S. Irvine Vol 7839/108 consolidated lots 6,7,8 & 9

1985 Richard & Joyce Godfrey

Lot 8

1892 Robert Blair paid £6.3s for 1.25 acres

1908 Margaret McDonald

1919 Thomas Shaw

1924 Arthur Keith Urquhart

1953 J.M. & J.S. Irvine Vol 9694/337 consolidated lots 6,7,8 & 9

1986 William & Shirley Biffin

1997 Ivan & Lynette Voss – PS417486V subdivided into 4 lots

Lot 9 – North side of Joanna Street

1893 William Irwin paid £5 6/5 for 1.25 acres

1900 Thomas Burt

1909 Charles MacGillivray

1909 Margaret MacKenzie

1919 Thomas Shaw (son of earlier Thomas Shaw of Wooriwyrite)

1924 Arthur Keith Urquhart

1953 J.M. & J.S. Irvine Vol 9377/846 consolidated lots 6,7,8 & 9

1980 Peter Holbeach

Lot 10 – South side of Joanna Street

1916 James Irvine (hotelkeeper) paid £40 for 2.25 acres

1918 Thomas Turner Shaw

1924 Arthur Keith Urquhart

1953 Marjorie Holbeach (died 1965)

1968 William (died 1981) & Peter Holbeach

1981 Peter Holbeach

Lot 11

1916 Charles Ogilvie from Cobden paid £12 for 1.75 acres

1918 Thomas Turner Shaw part Vol 4163/418

1924 Arthur Keith Urquhart

1953 Marjorie Holbeach

1968 William "Bill" (died 1981) & Peter Holbeach

1981 Peter Holbeach

Part Vol 5182/235

1926 Charles Callaway

Lot 12 – North of J.M. Irvine Reserve

1916 Charles Callaway paid £25 for 1.5 acres

1925 Arthur Keith Urquhart

1953 Marjorie Holbeach

1968 William & Peter Holbeach

1981 Peter Holbeach

Peter Holbeach Properties – 2002

Lot 9   1.25 acres

Lot 10 2.25 acres

Lot 11 1.75 acres

Lot 12 1.5 acres

TOTAL APPROX 7 ACRES

Lot 2 Section B

1883 Mary Jane Irwin (died 1892) paid £20

1884 1894 Charles MacGillivray

1908 James Irvine

1920 James George Irvine & Ester Irvine

1938 James George Irvine

1969 J.M. & J.S. Irvine Vol 8803/637

1969 J.S. Irvine

Lot 3 Section B Vol 2602/333

1887 James Allen (Port Campbell grazier) paid £32 for 20 acres

1891 William Irwin

1908 Charles MacGillivray

1908 James Irvine

1919 James George Irvine & Esther Irvine

1938 James George Irvine

1969 J.M. & J.S. Irvine

1969 J.S. Irvine

Lot 4 Section B Vol 2062/334

1887 James Allen paid £18 for 9 acres

1894 William Irwin

1908 James Irvine (Licensed victualler)

1919 James George Irvine & Esther Irvine

1938 James George Irvine

1969 J.M. & J.S. Irvine

1969 J.S. Irvine

Lots 16-28 Section B Vol 2606/035

1893 James Irvine (Grazier) paid £247 7/6 for 34.5 acres

Excision from Lot 23 Vol 8112/992

1956 Ernest Wilson (Cobden)

1969 James Winchcombe

1975 John Irvine

1975 Rosalind Stansmore

Lot 21 Corner Irvine & Charles Streets Subdivided

1989 M. & R. Moroney Vol 9783/052

1987 J.S. Irvine Vol 9782/055

1987 J.S. Irvine Vol 9783/056

Lot 28 Corner Hamilton & Irvine Streets

1969 J.S. Irvine

1974 Ray Willox

1979 William Burl

1990 Particia Burl

Lot 23 – Corner Cumming & Hamilton Streets – part

1975 Loma Pescott Vol 9083/181

1995 Graham & Dorothy Little

Lot 23 – Next to Corner Lot Cumming Street

1979 Roger Pescott Vol 9340/867

1995 Meryl Hayden

Lot 23 – Halladale Road, Hamilton Street,Cumming Street & Endin-
burgh Castle Road - remainder subdivided into 3 lots LP139377 – 2 on
Halladale Road & limestone depression

Lot 25 Hamilton Street – part subdivided

1985 D. & C. Nisbet Vol 9462/997

1985 R. & E. Schouller Vol 9642 999

1985 A.R. & P. Ongarello Vol 9693/650

Lot 27 – "Moness" Vol 8989/108

J.S Irvine three parts & Elizabeth Stephens one part

1980 J.S. Irvine

1999 Katherine & Ronald Irvine

Lots 22, 24, 25 & 26 – Corner Hamilton, Cumming & Charles Streets
Subdivided PS323405 – 5 lots

Lot 31 Vol 5290/828

1923 Robert Dorey pair £30 for 2.5 acres

SUBDIVIDED

1951 Dorothy (died 1974) & Ben Richards (Died 1969) Vol 7522/176

1974 Alfred Richards

1990 Warrnambool Shire Council

1951 Dorothy & Ben Richards Vol 7522/177

1974 Alfred Richards

1990 Warrnambool Shire Council

1957 Susan & Francis Neal Vol 7522/178

1961 T & L Lock

1996 Phillip Lock

1951 Flora & George Richards Vol 7522/179

1967 Tom & Bev Lynch

1951 Mabel & Leslie Rentell

1963 R. Parlour

1983 A., G., J., J., M., R. & J. Parlour

1951 Cyril Couch

1964 C. & U. Sharp

1968 R. & J. Woods

1987 D. & L. Fraser

Peterborough history – rural property

West side of Curdies River

Crown allotment 106 5973/544 – this is all the land from Great Ocean Road between MacGillivray Streets and the Warrnambool Road including the Casino and Childers Streets development north to about the current rubbish tip site.

1935 Lily Ann Blair – 194 acres – £146.5s - original title

1935 Thomas Griffin Vol 6002/303 - 19 acres

1959 Mary Jane Blair 175 acres

1951 T.Moyle Breton

    7932/133 to E Tucker & E Chapple

    8020/018 1953

    8070/602 1954 CRB

    8240/526 1954 Andrew Sproat – Corner MacGillivray & GOR

    8889/402 1971 Barry Jenkins – 15 acres – Casino & Childers Street subdivision.

Transferred to Chandos Investments Pty Ltd in 1971

Vol 8934/718 – 1 lot in Casino Street

Vol 8934/797 – 30 lots in Casino & Childers Streets

Vol 9338/057 1979 G Paton & Ila Murnane – 1979

Vol 10020/805 1990 Barry Jenkins – 3.276 hectares

Vol 10020/806 Bourke & Loader

Vol 9210/870 Ian Jarvis – Crown Allotment106a

Jemima Robertson's property

Between 1875 and 1882 Jemima purchased 9 acres (18 lots) of Sections 2, 3 and 5 in the Township surveyed area, 47 acres of Crown Allotment 104a (west side of CA 106) and originally bought by William Herring for £48 in 1881. This she donated to the Presbyterian Church in 1882 together with three half acre lots of Section 6 in the Township where the church was built. In addition she purchased:

> 6 acres CA "A" is part of Michael & Phoebe Moore's land.
>
> 20 acres – CA 3a fronting the Curdies Estuary north of Antares Street, paid £40
>
> 253 acres CA's 104, 105, 108b and 111 – originally purchased by Thomas Merrett in 1877 for £223. This land extended from where the Great Ocean Road and Merrett Street is now located to the north.
>
> 36 acres CA's 110b and 108b – north of the 223 acres above & fronting the Warrnambool Road on the south side.
>
> 450 acres CA's 65, 66, 66a, 67a, 80, 81, 82, 108a, 109, 110a and 109 all on the east side of the Warrnambool Road extending to the Curdies River & Estuary where the "Lodge Farm" is now located.
>
> The total area of all this land was approximately 792 acres. Most of the farm land was purchased from the Crown for £1 per acre. However, CA 81 & 82 & 109, 166 acres on

the Estuary, had been purchased from Alexander Patterson who was the owner for the three years prior. CA 80 51 acres (on the River) purchased from Archibald Eddington who was owner from 1870-75. Vol 438/419

She built *The Big House* in Blair Street in 1874. She died in 1884 and her executors carried on with all the property until 1890 when her son Alexander became the owner. Unfortunately, by 1895, the whole of the 710 acres of the farm had passed to the Bank of Australasia and the Township properties had all been sold to Helen Blair who carried on the guest house business under the *Blair Athol* name. It is likely, her nephew Alexander Robertson, became a victim of the 1890s financial crash and this seemed to end the Robertson connection with Peterborough.

In 1896, James Arthur Robilliard purchased part of the Robertson farm from the Bank of Australasia. In 1909 he sold the 450 acres on the east side of the Warrnambool Road to James Irvine and the 259 acres on the west side in 1910 to Charles MacGillivray & Tom McKenzie.

Other land owners on west side of Curdies River

Crown Allotment 102 Vol 5973/544

Lily Ann Blair – 194 acres – £156

The Croft family originally purchased 464 acres north from Croft's Bay CA's 116,115a,b&c,112a&b,113a&b & 117a

Crown Allotment 102 Vol 1237/223

1881 Henry Croft 113 acres – paid £114

Margaret Campbell purchased 172 acres, CA 78a in 1941 for £49 (on Warrnambool Road) died 10 November 1960

Crown Allotment 77a Vol 6258/596

1938 Ruth Victoria Blair 129 acres – paid £65 (near Bay of Islands)

Irvine Brothers CA 107 (51 acres on River) Ca 107 107 acres near Bay of Islands

CA's 72, 71a,67b,79a,117b over 900 acres in all

Three 20 acres River frontage lots north of the Antares Street

2a 1885 Henry Croft

3a 1876 Jemima Robertson

1a 1888 S.Tarrington

East side of Curdies Estuary

1981 Robert Blair CA11 16 acres on Peterborough Timboon Road Vol 1254/744

1890 Sam Valentine

1892 G. Valentine

1905 Charles MacGillivray

1935 M. MacKenzie, S. Milne and M. Nieman

1881 Charles MacGillivray (address Port Campbell) CA 5 18 acres on Peterborough Timboon Road paid £63 Vol 1275/822

1935 M.MacKenzie, S.Milne, M. Nieman

24.

1881 Charles MacGillivray CA 6, 20 acres on Peterborough Timboon Road paid £16 Vol 1427/321

1935 M. MacKenzie, S. Milne and M. Nieman

1884 Charles MacGillivray CA 10 Vol 1574/753 on Peterborough Timboon Road.

1935 M. MacKenzie, S. Milne and M. Nieman

1935 M. MacKenzie, S. Milne and M. Nieman owned CA's 5, 6, 10 and 11 – 74 acres

1966 Purchased by Alan and Ian Jarvis Vol 5990/925

1873 James Thwaites CA 96 and 97 Vol 6346/189

1883 William Allen of Allansford

1946 Jessie Cochrane CA 86 & 86a 597 acres Vol 6756/109 & Vol 1018/451

1959 Gordon Cumming

1939 Jessie Cochrane and Thomas Cumming CA's 96, 97, 98, 99, 100, 102.534 acres paid £2246

1909 Rod Urquhart of Hexham and Fred Redford CA 83 82 acres paid £83 (on River)

1910 J. Dance

1910 Fred Croft

1944 Allan, William and Fred Croft Vol 6628/936

1949 William Croft Vol 7319/723 and Vol 8623/501

1889 Robert Blair 194 acres (on River) CA's 64a & 64b paid £195 Vol 2170/826 & 7.

INDEX